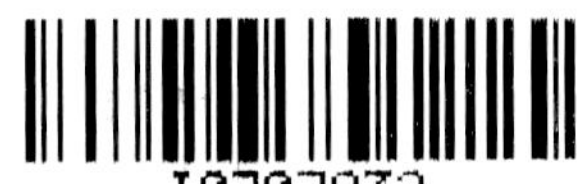
I0707932

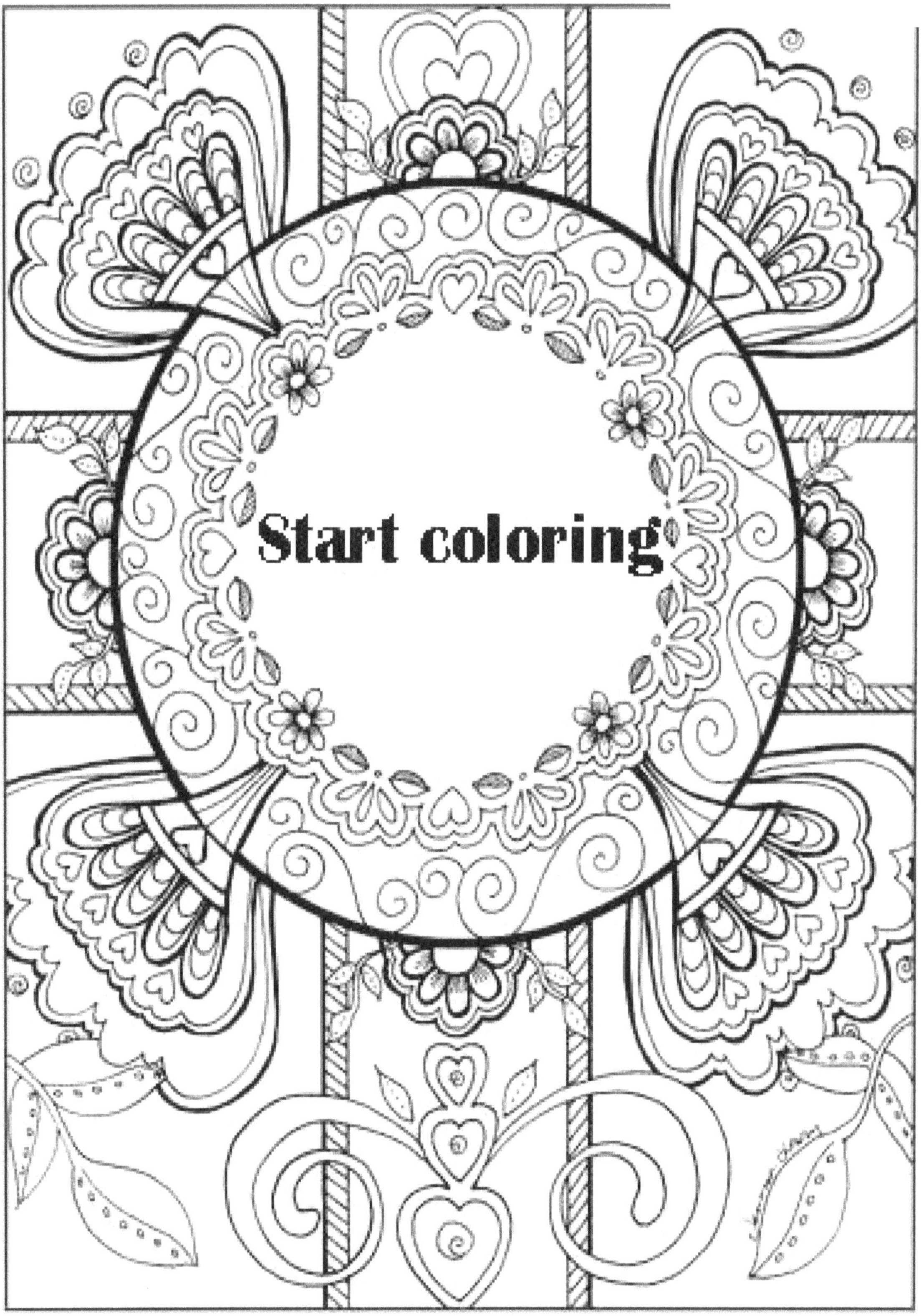

Start coloring

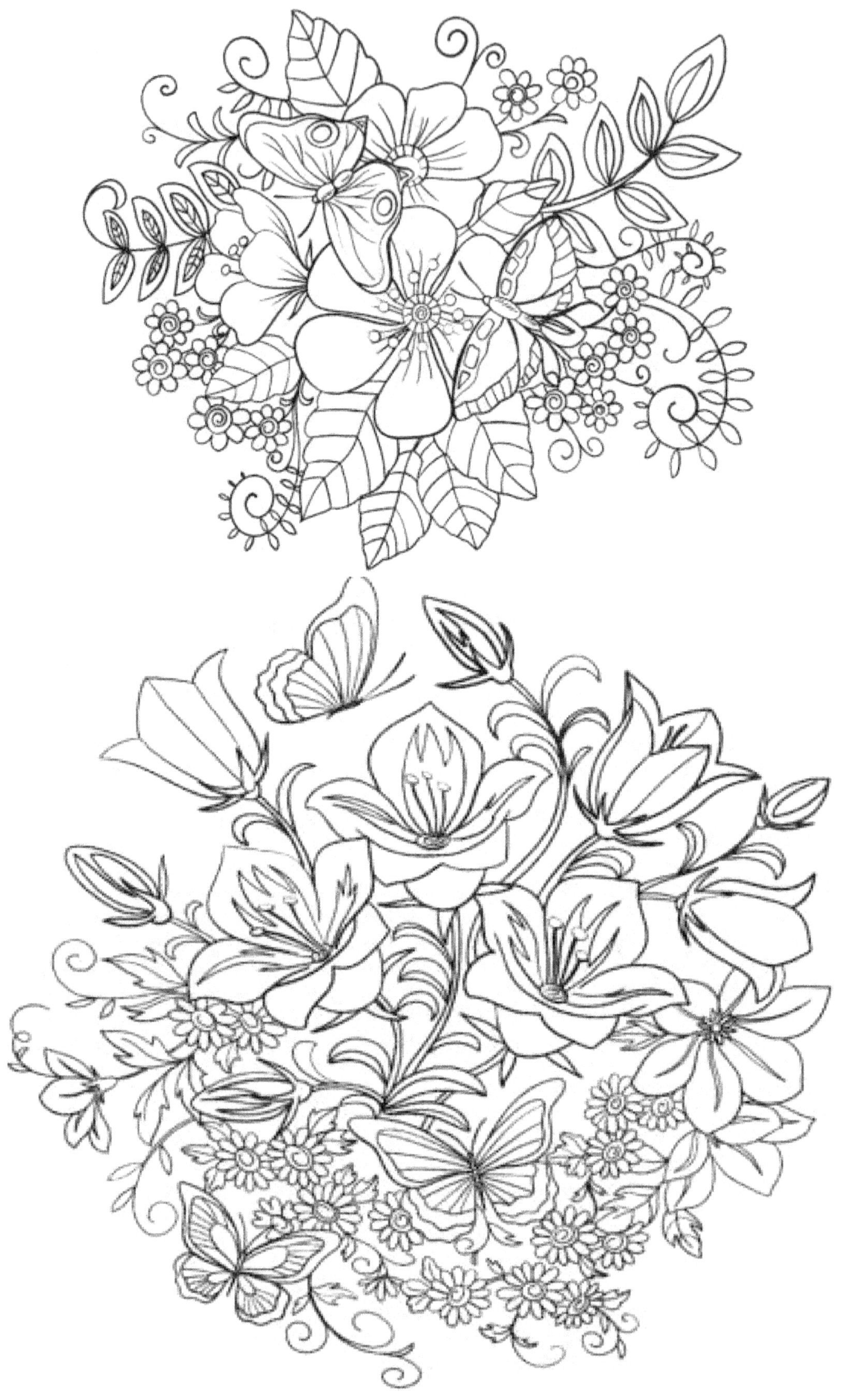

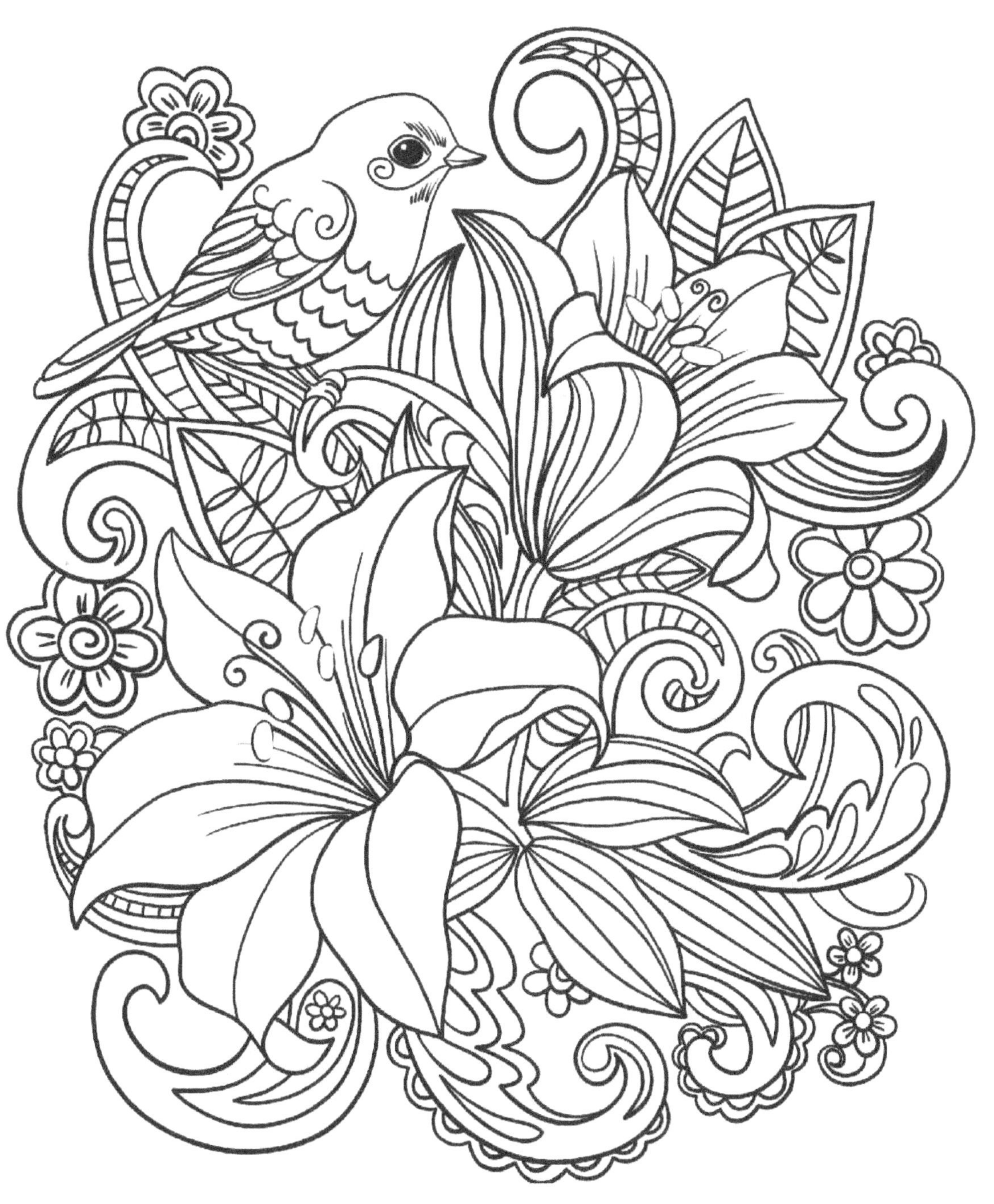

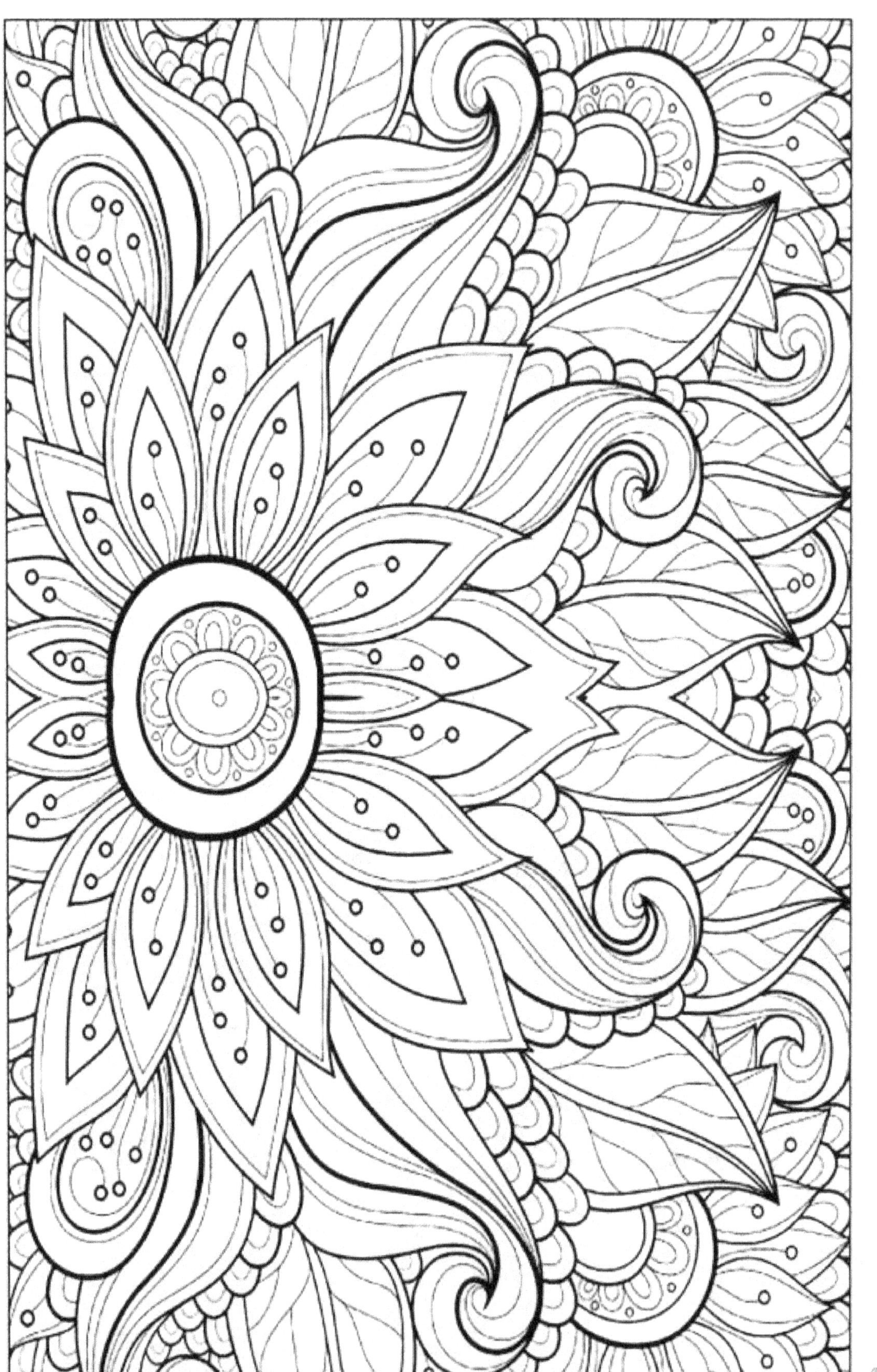

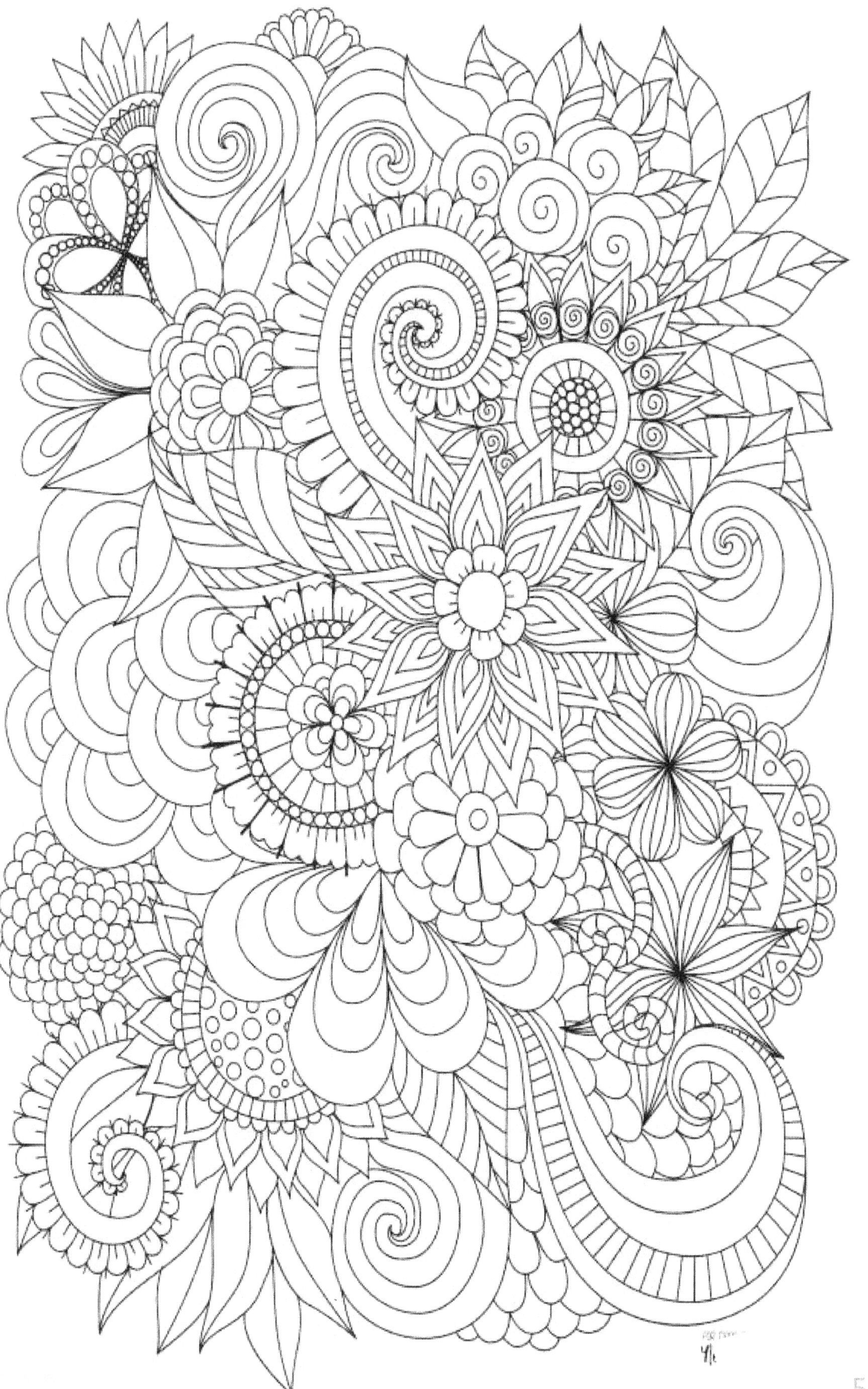

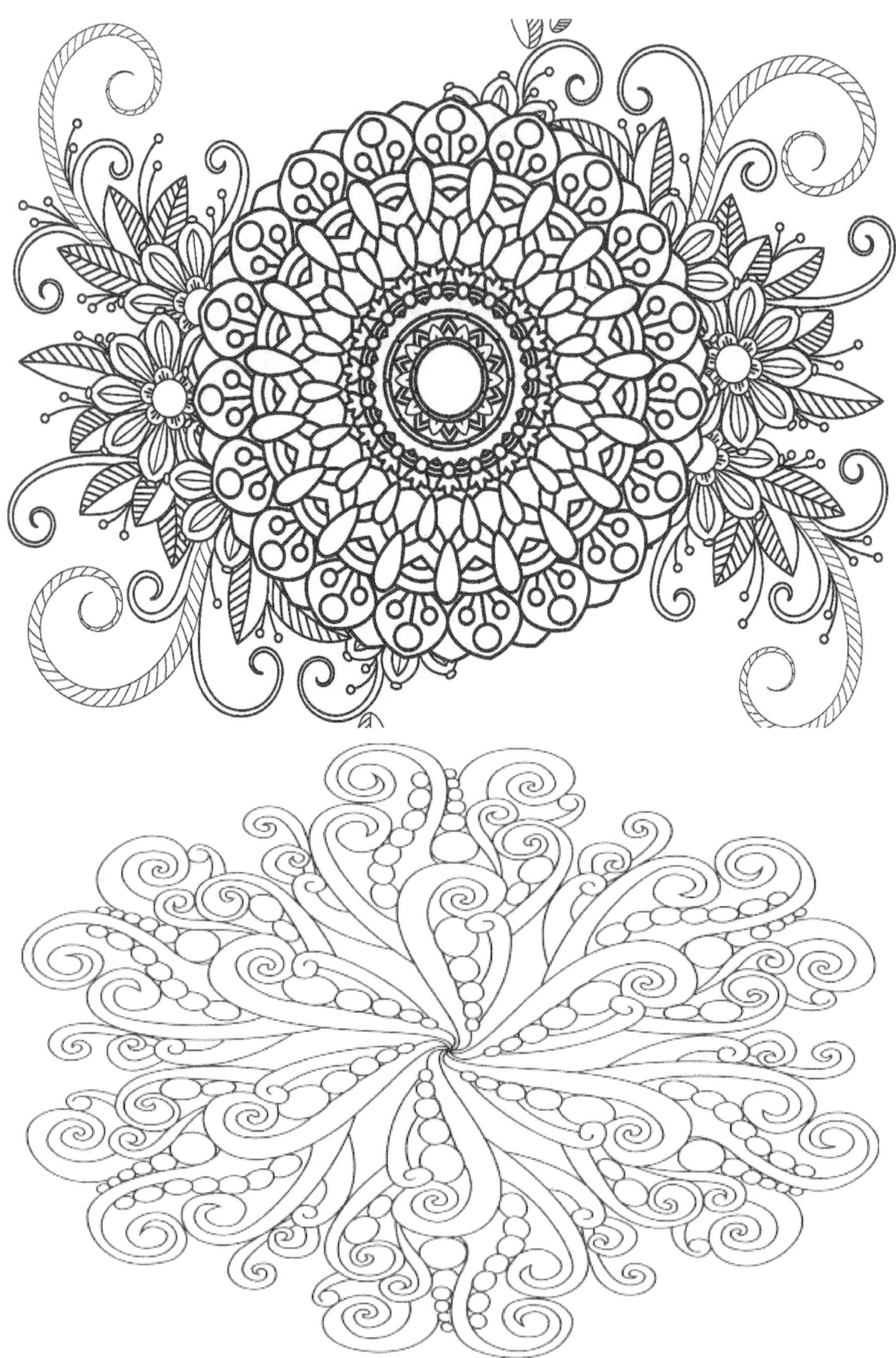

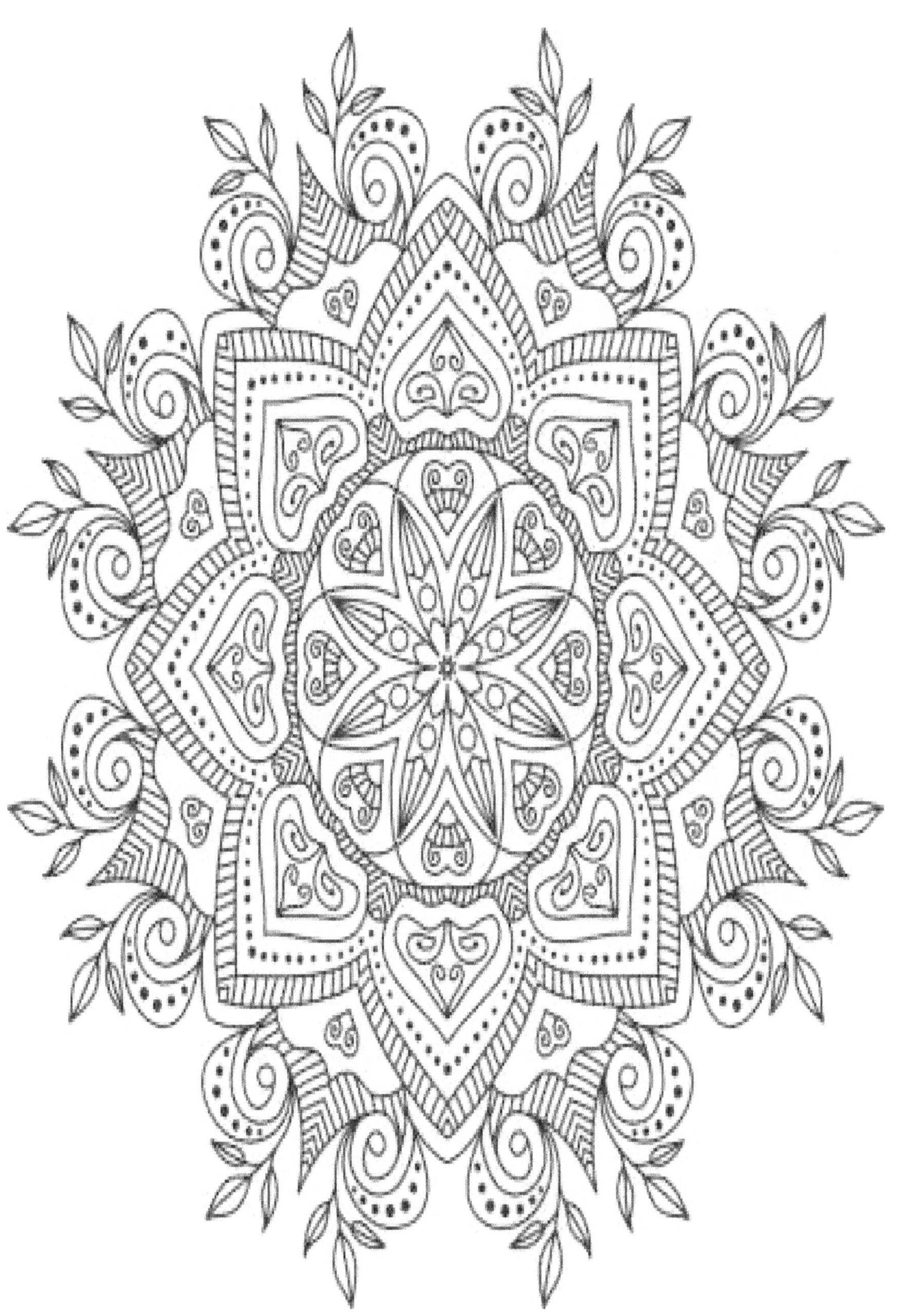

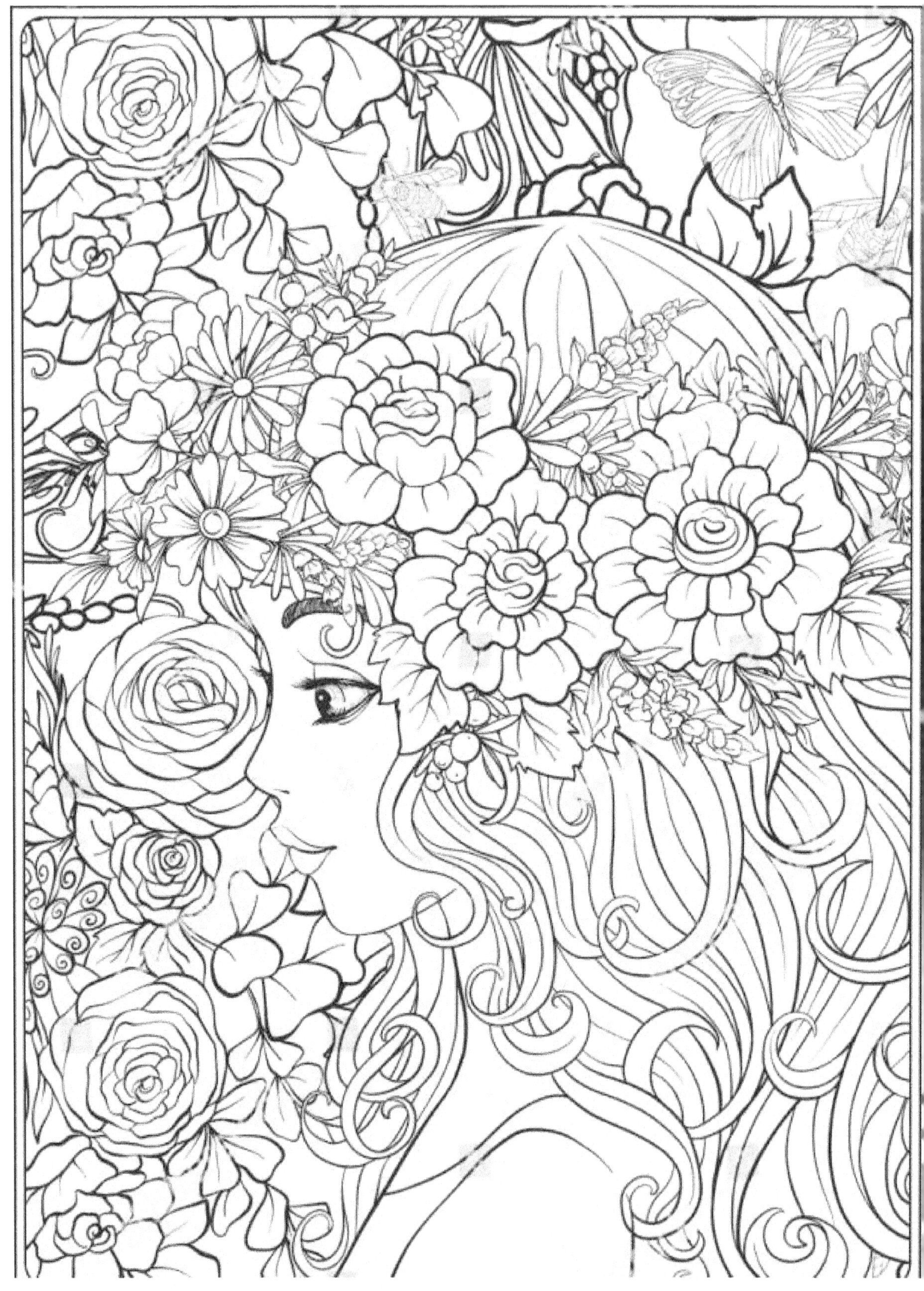

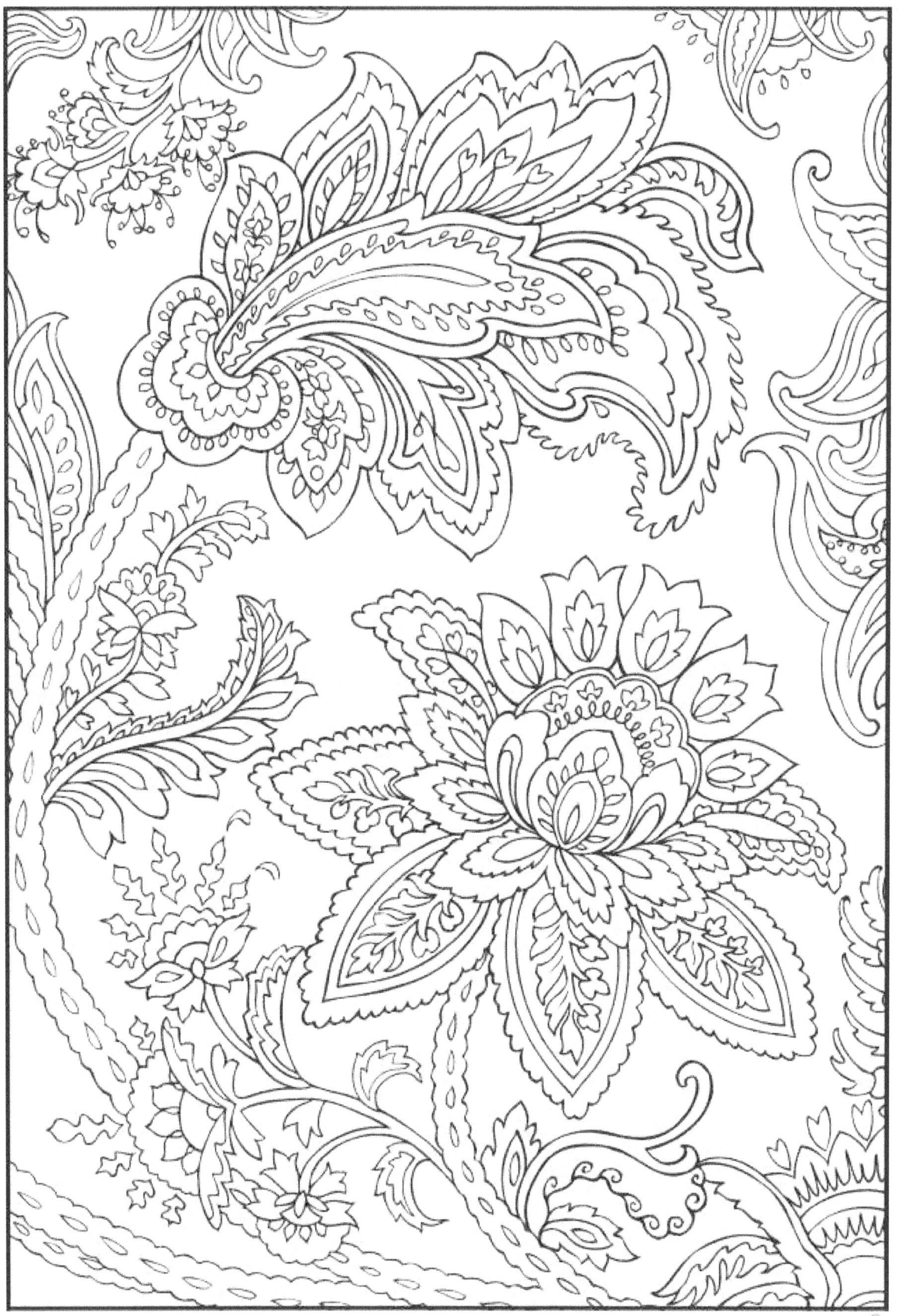

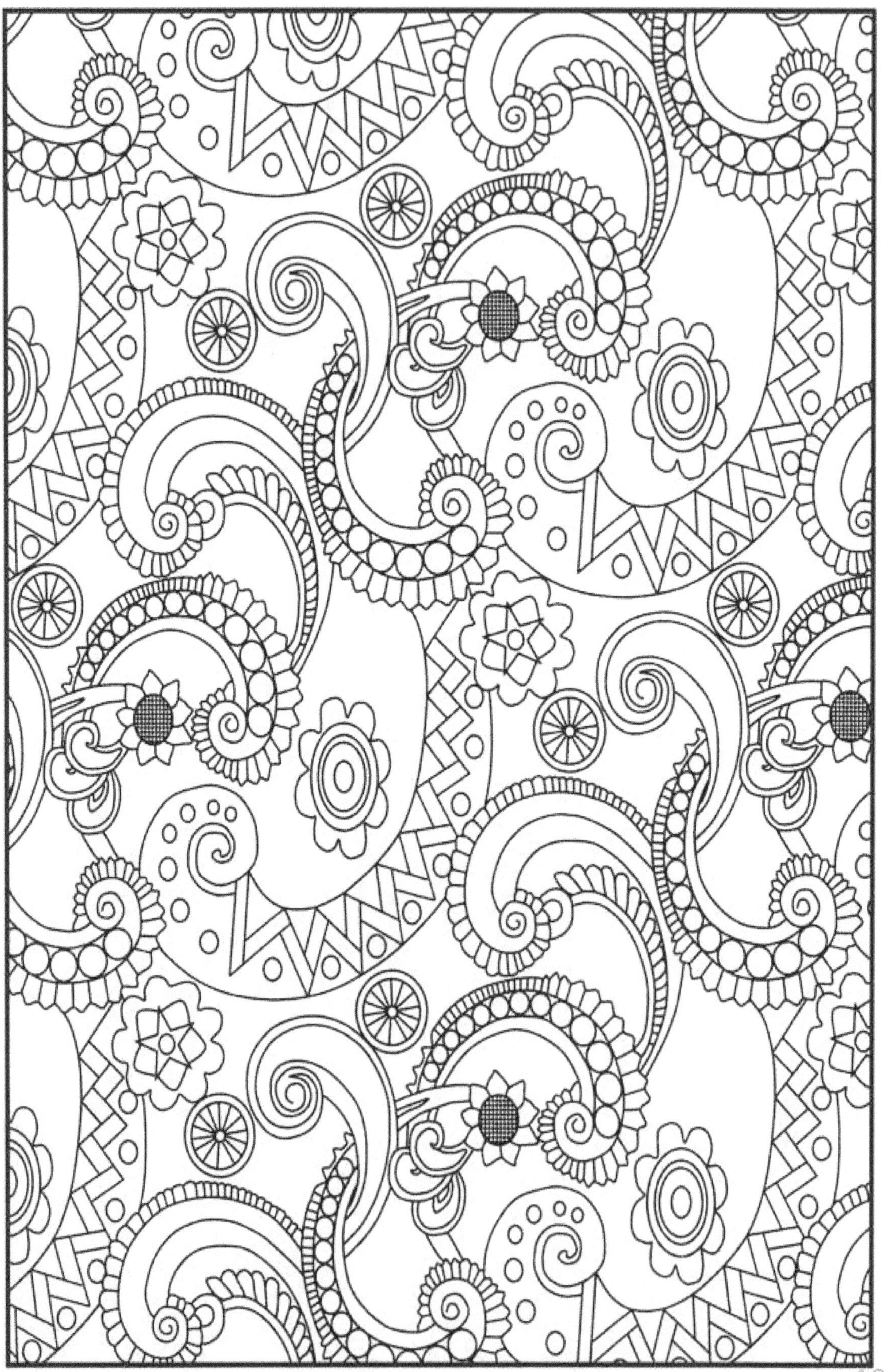

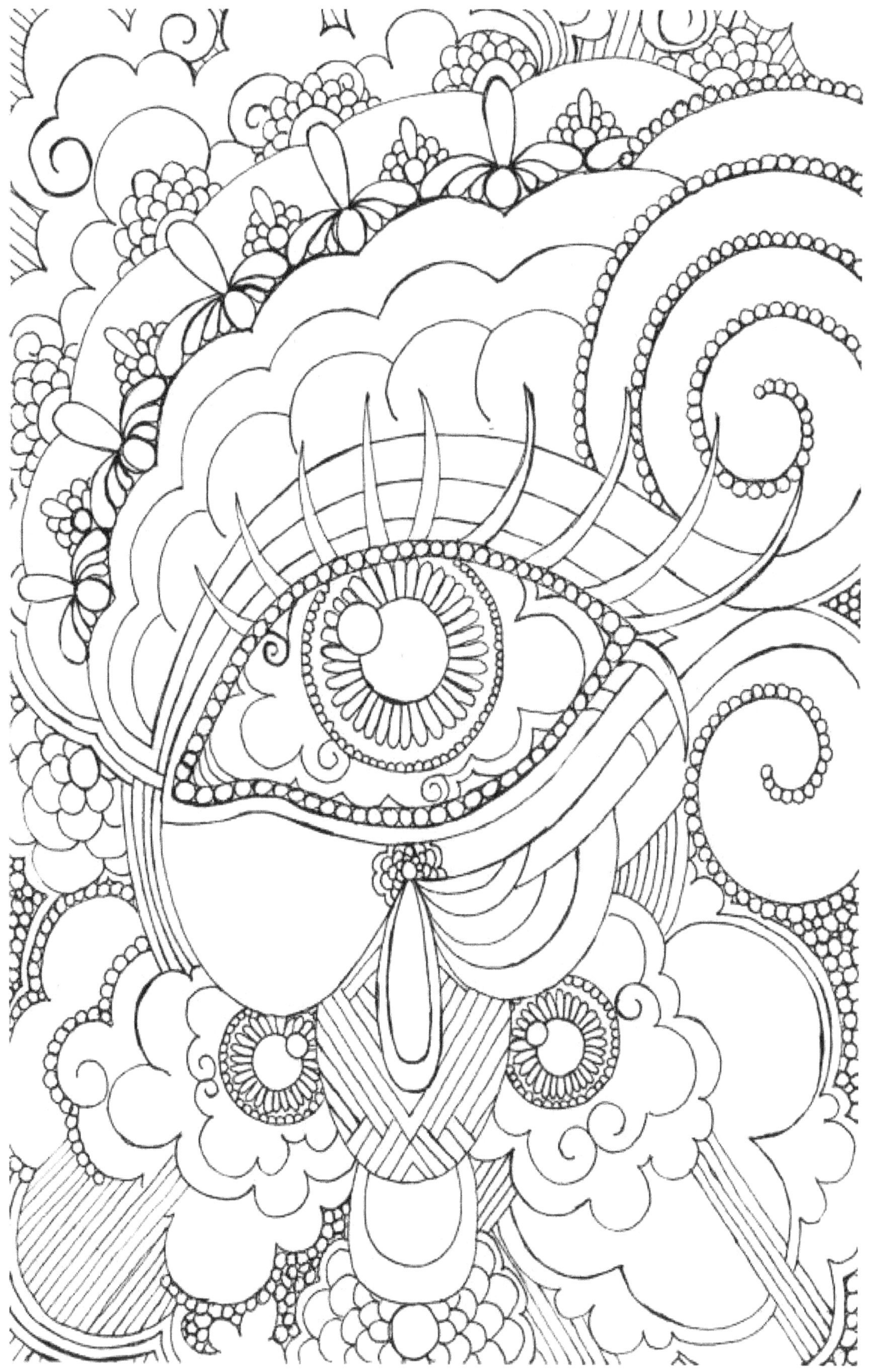

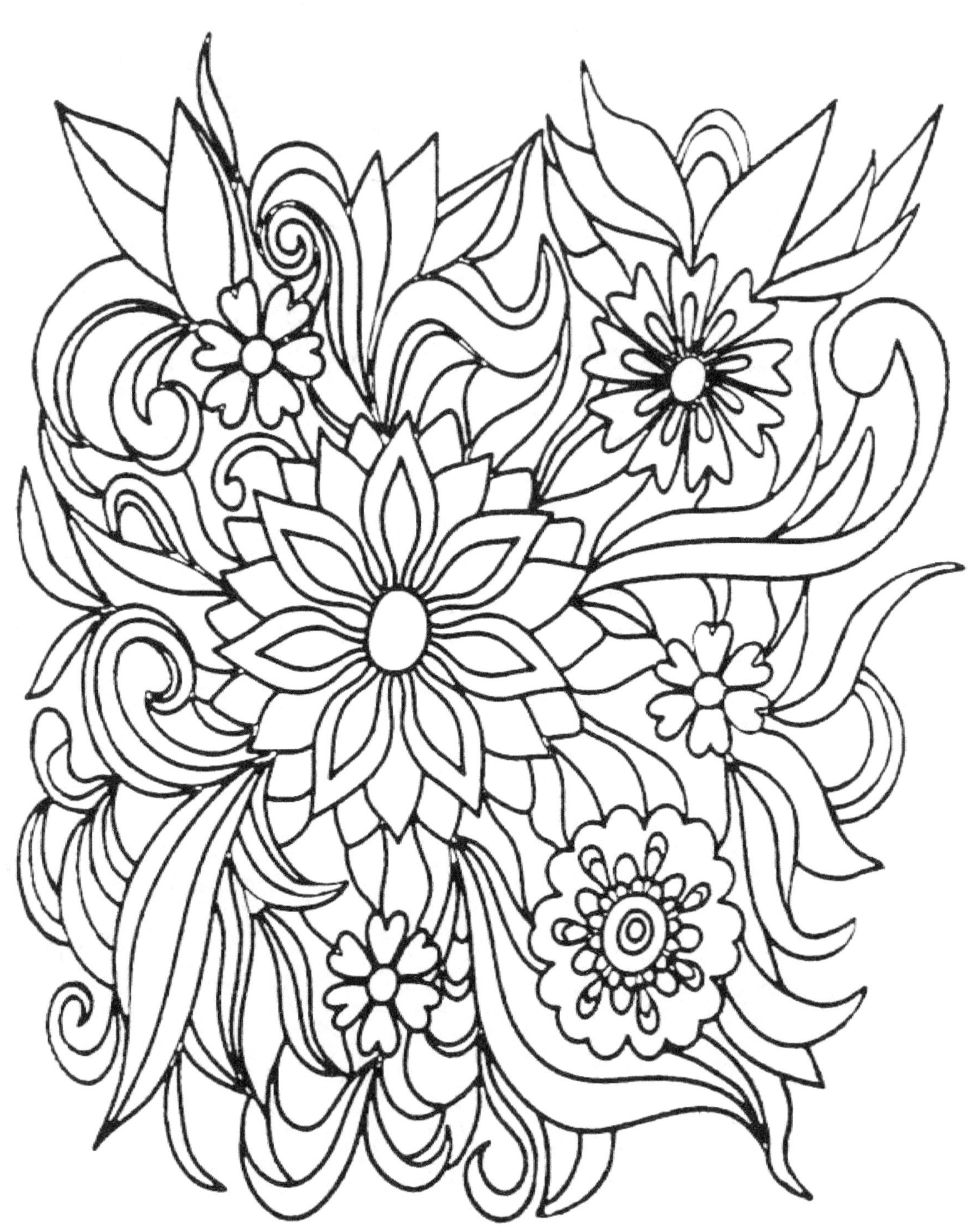

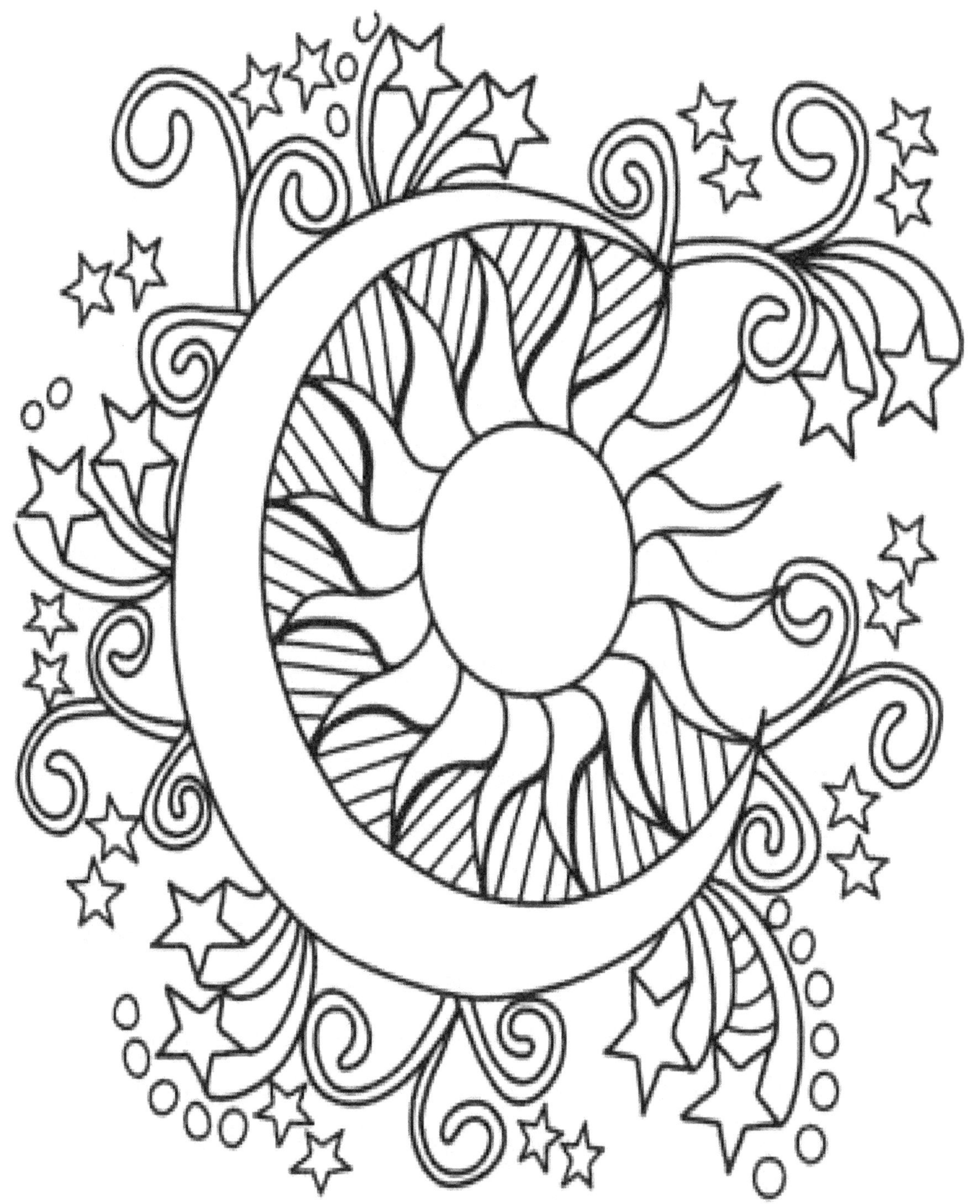

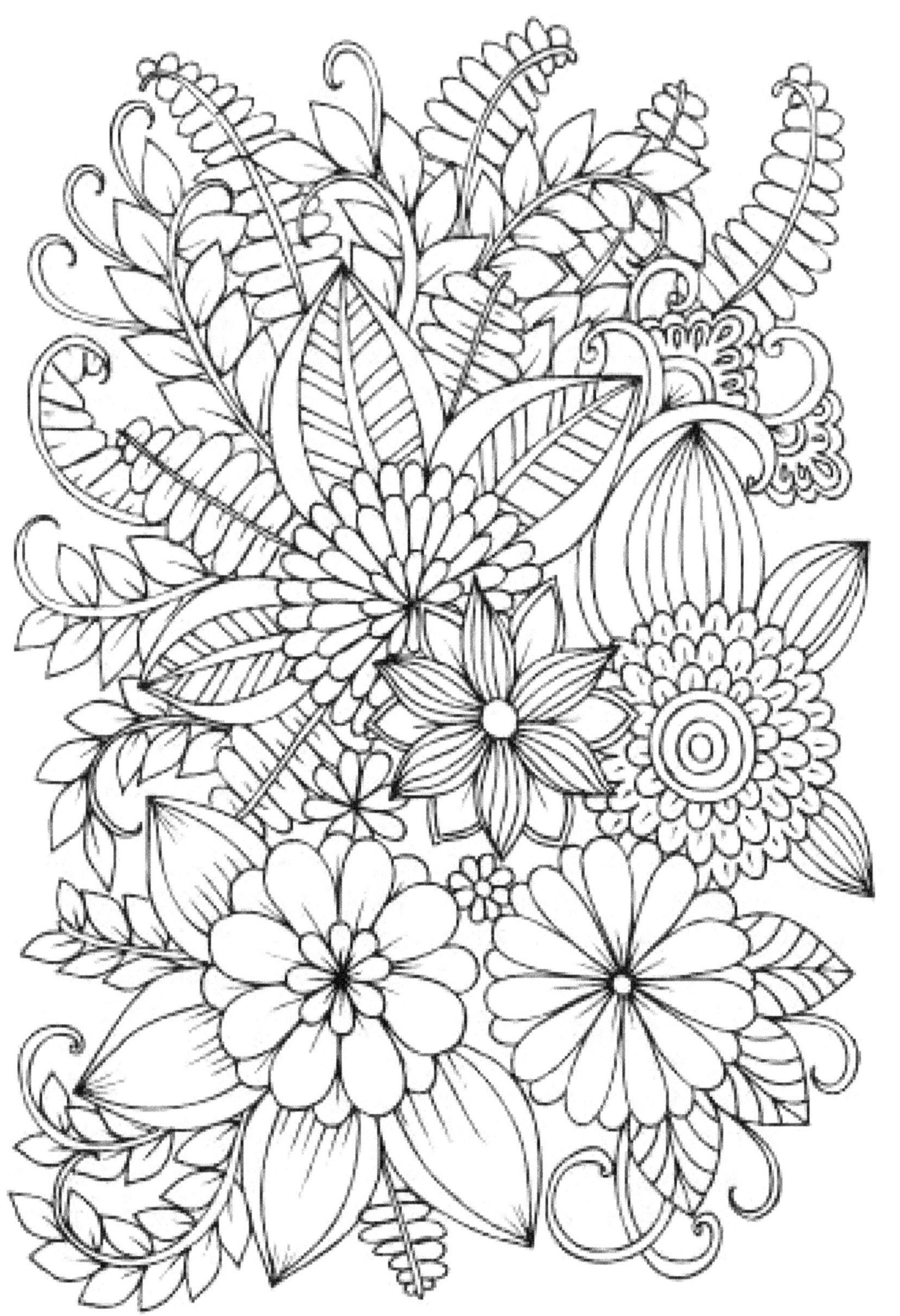

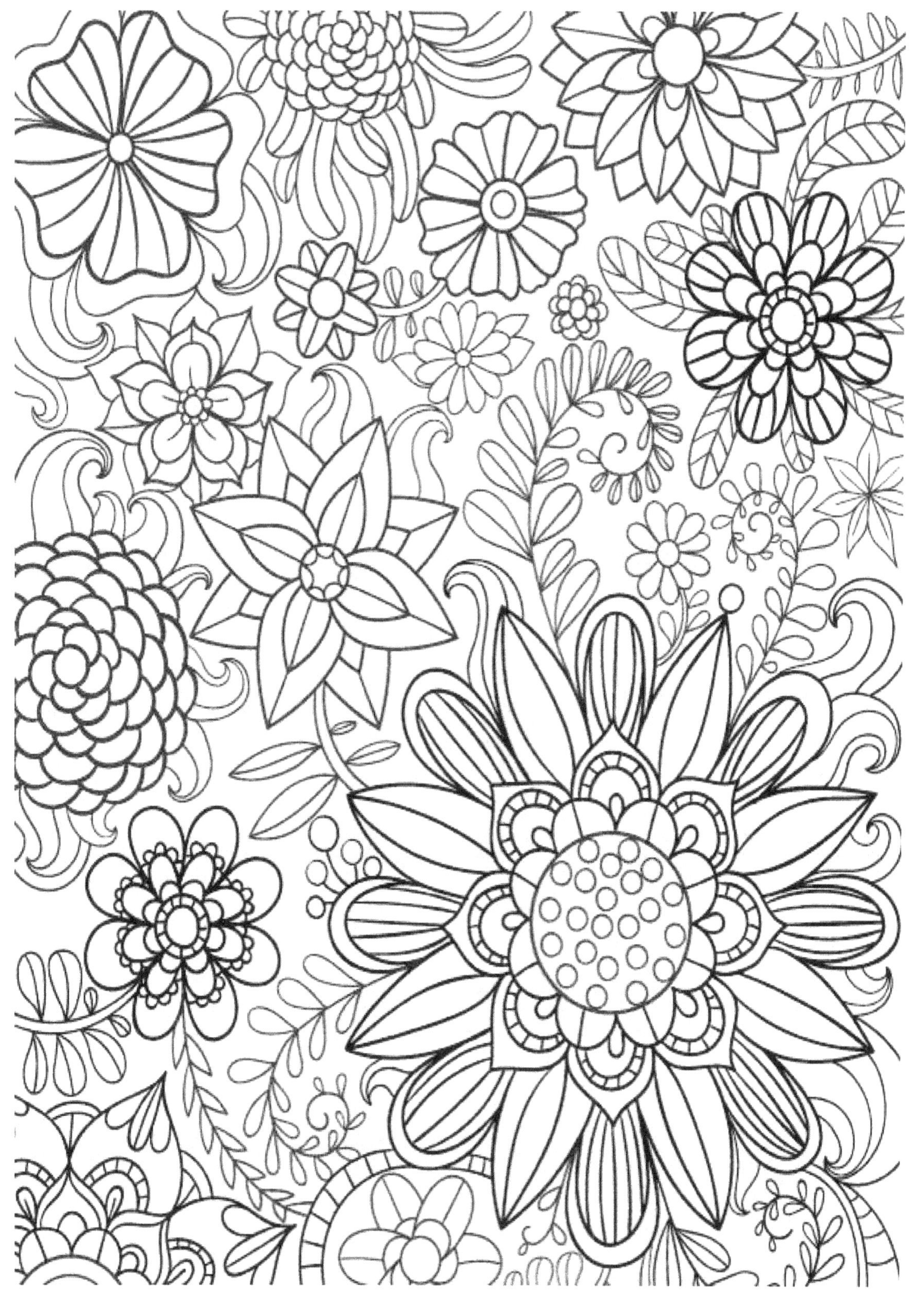

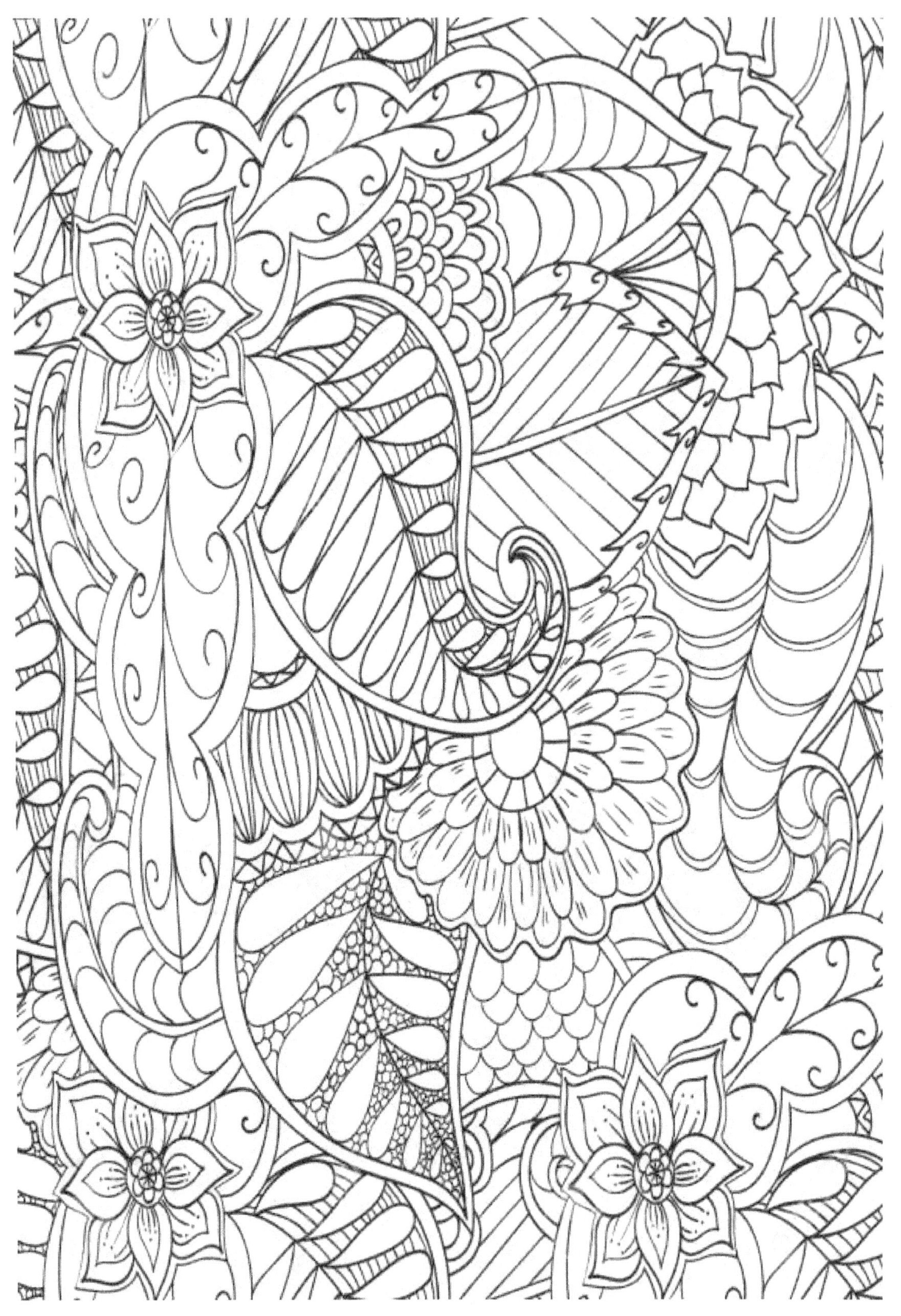

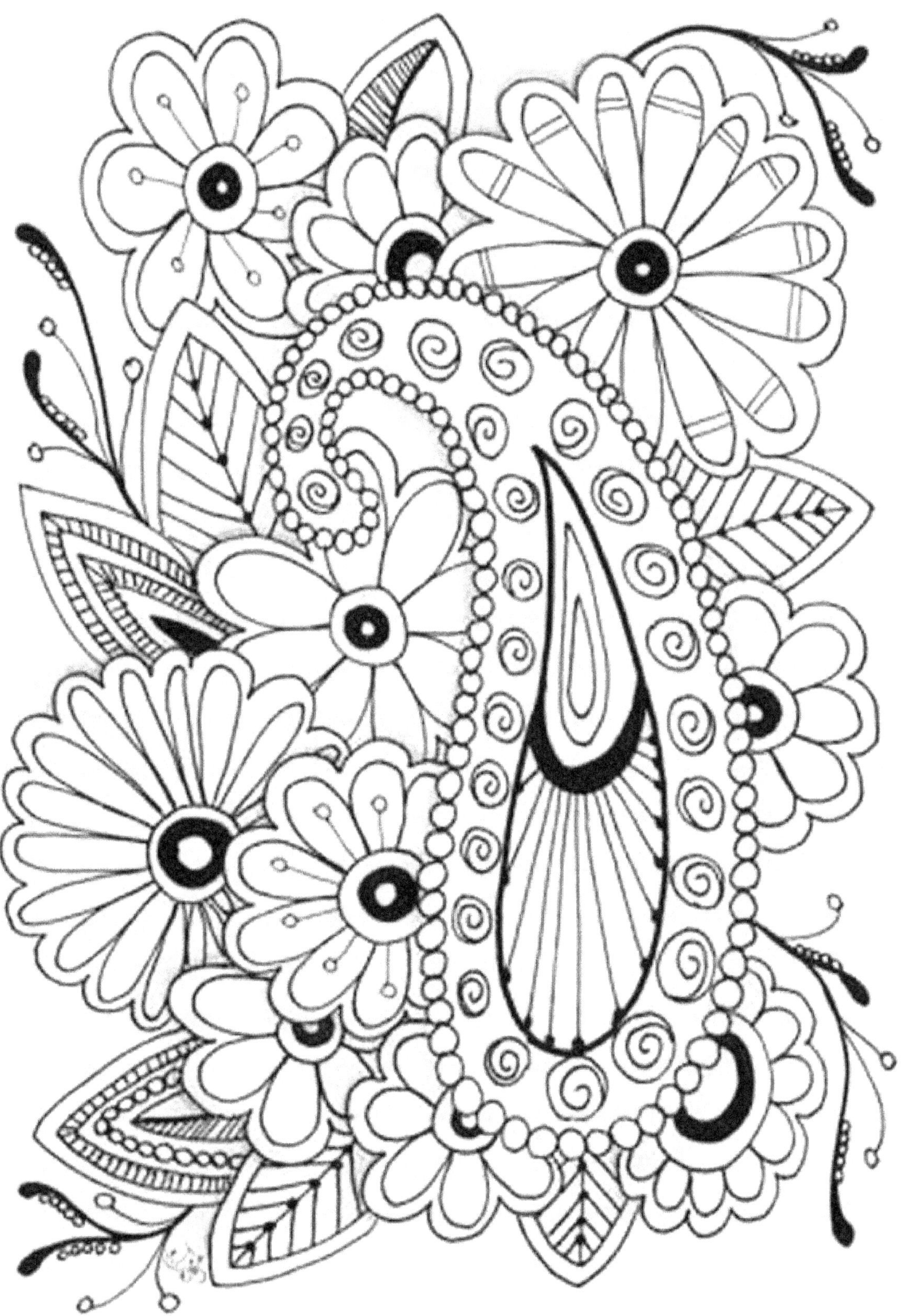

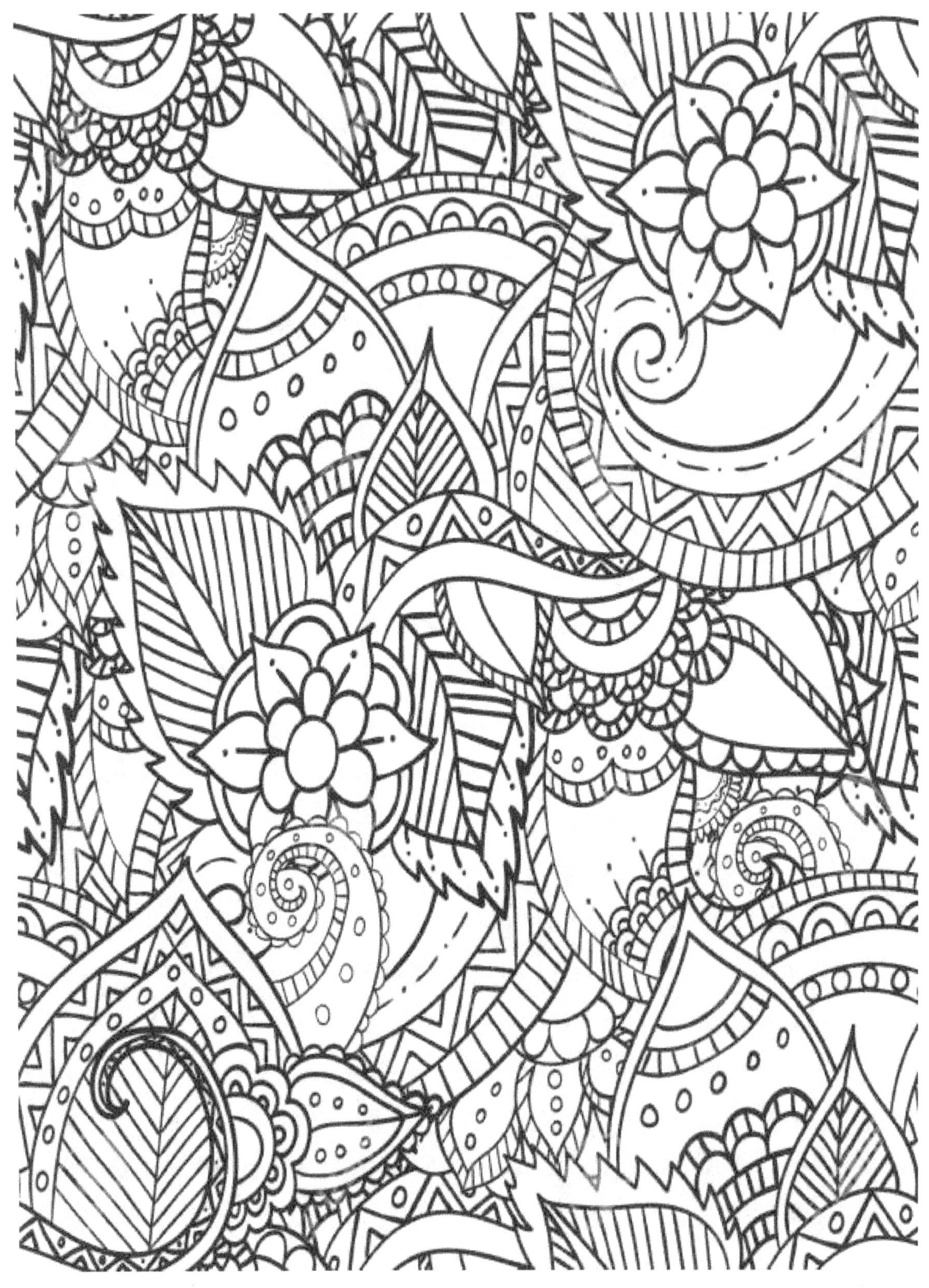

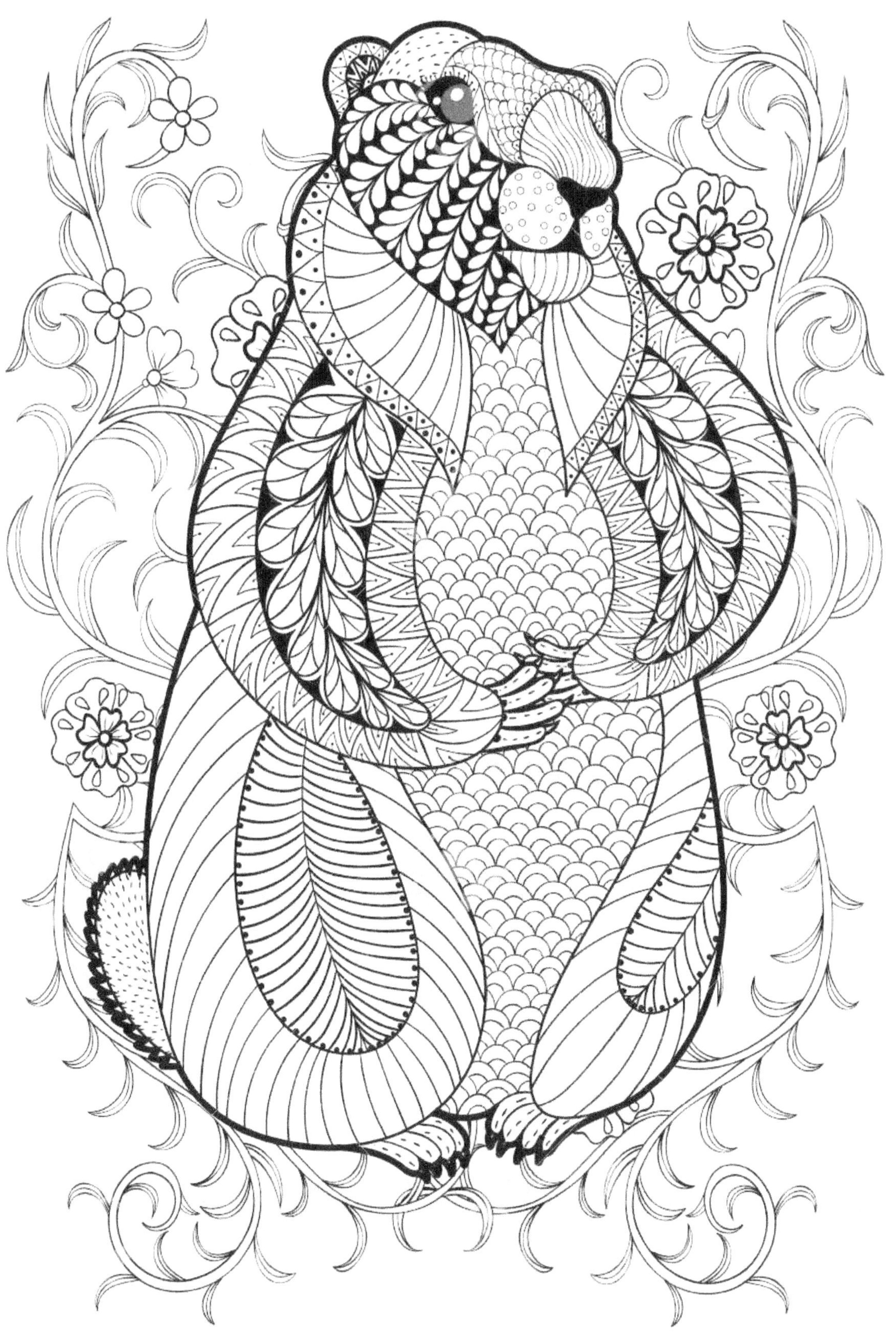

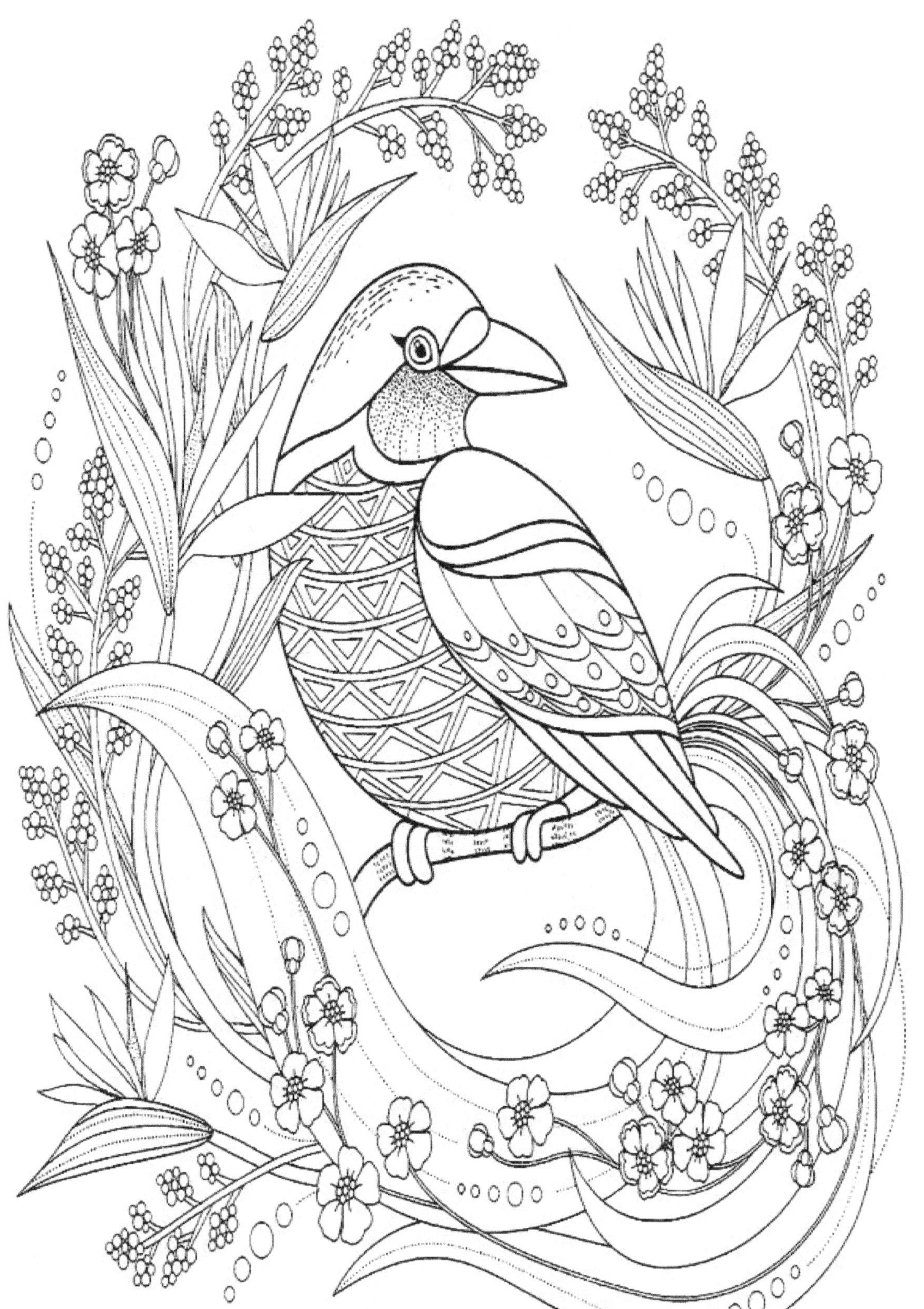

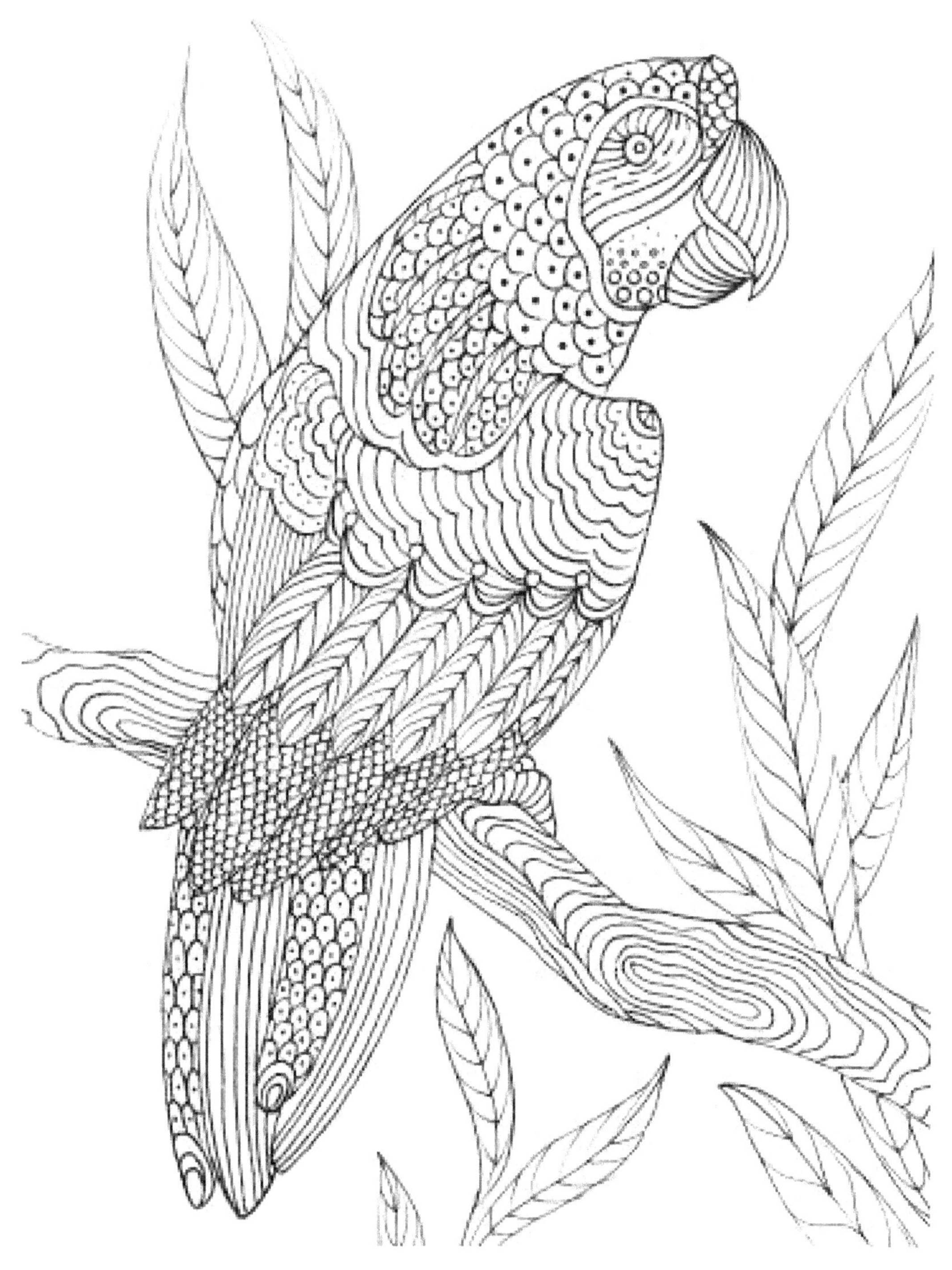

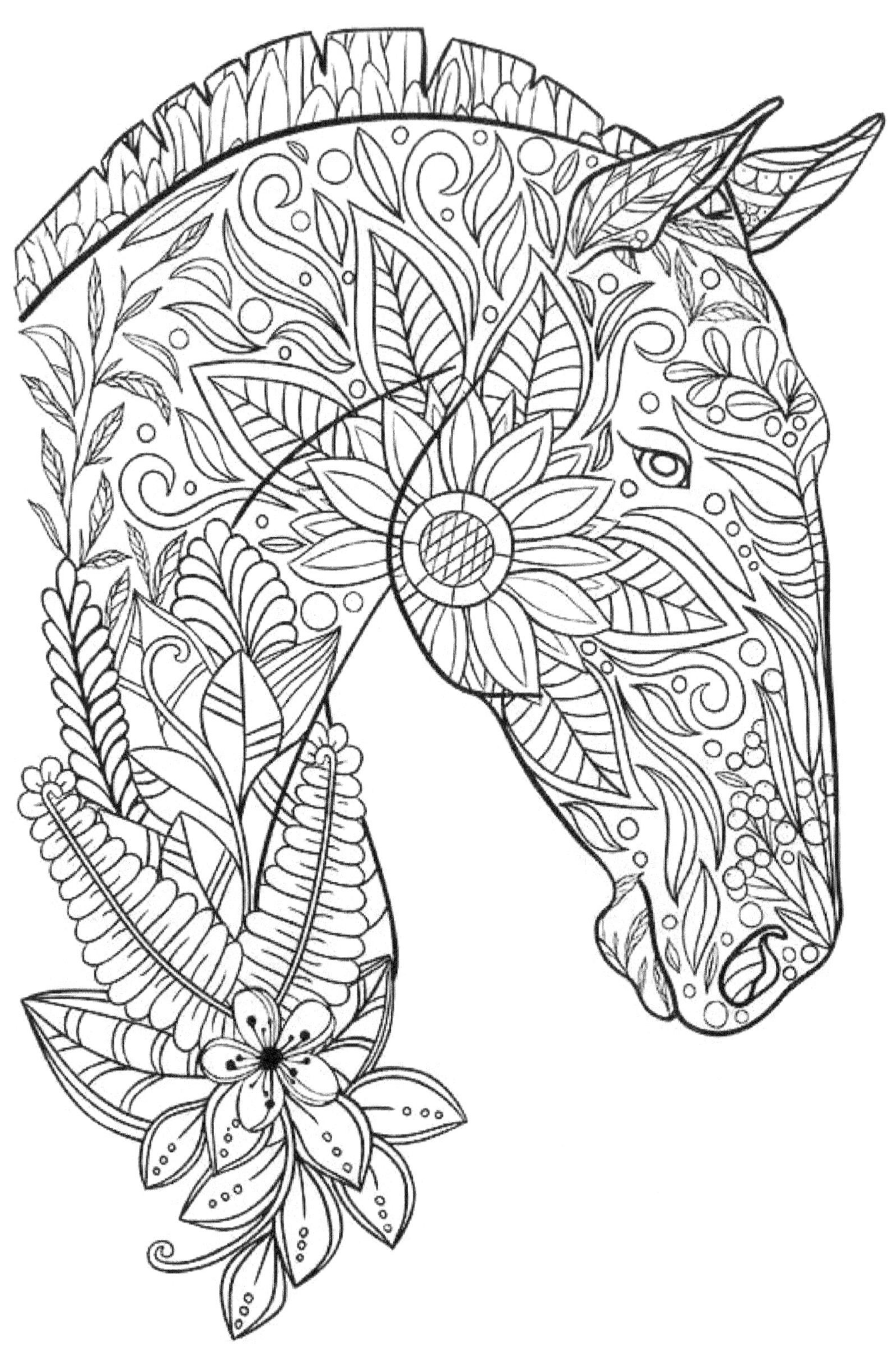

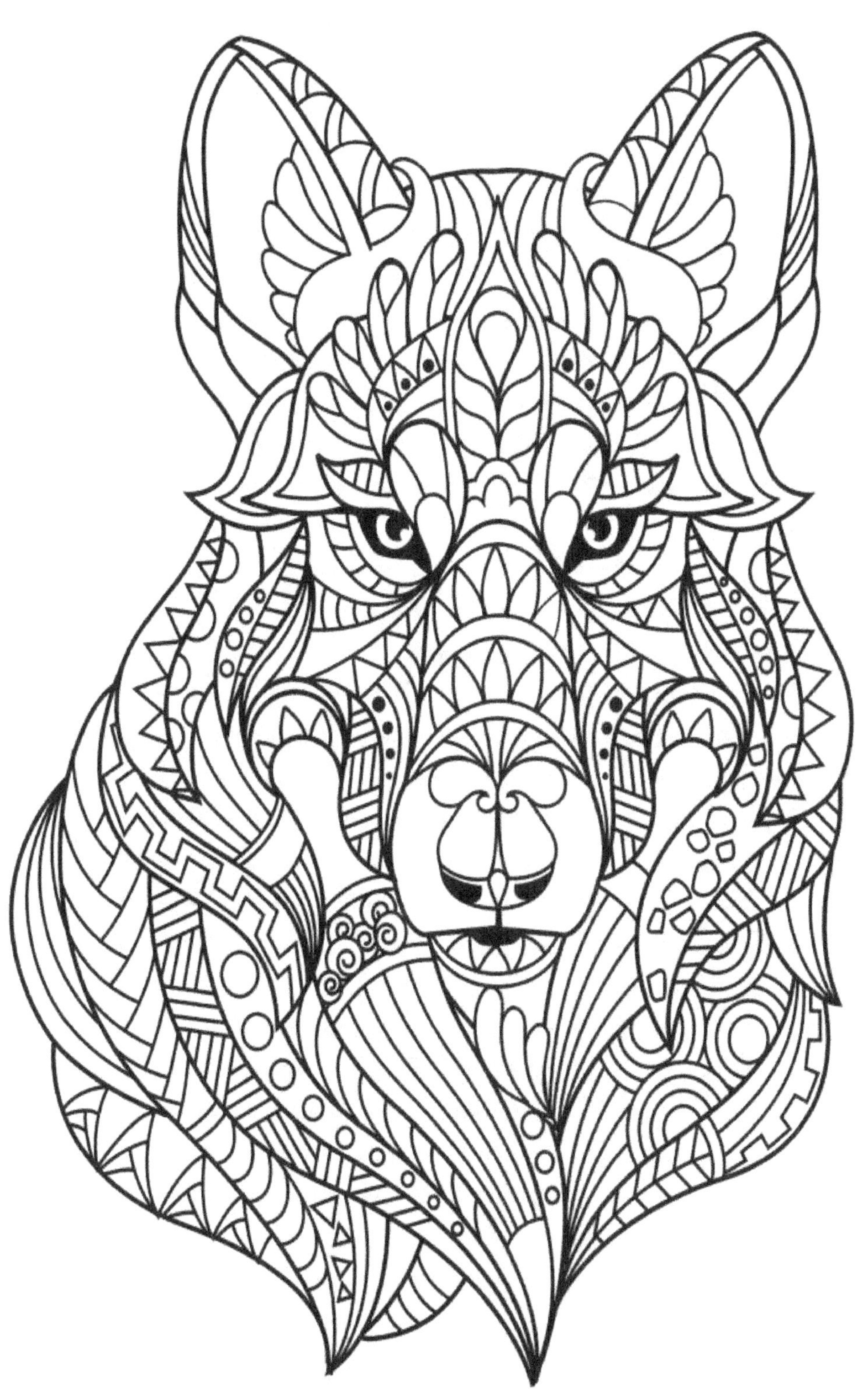

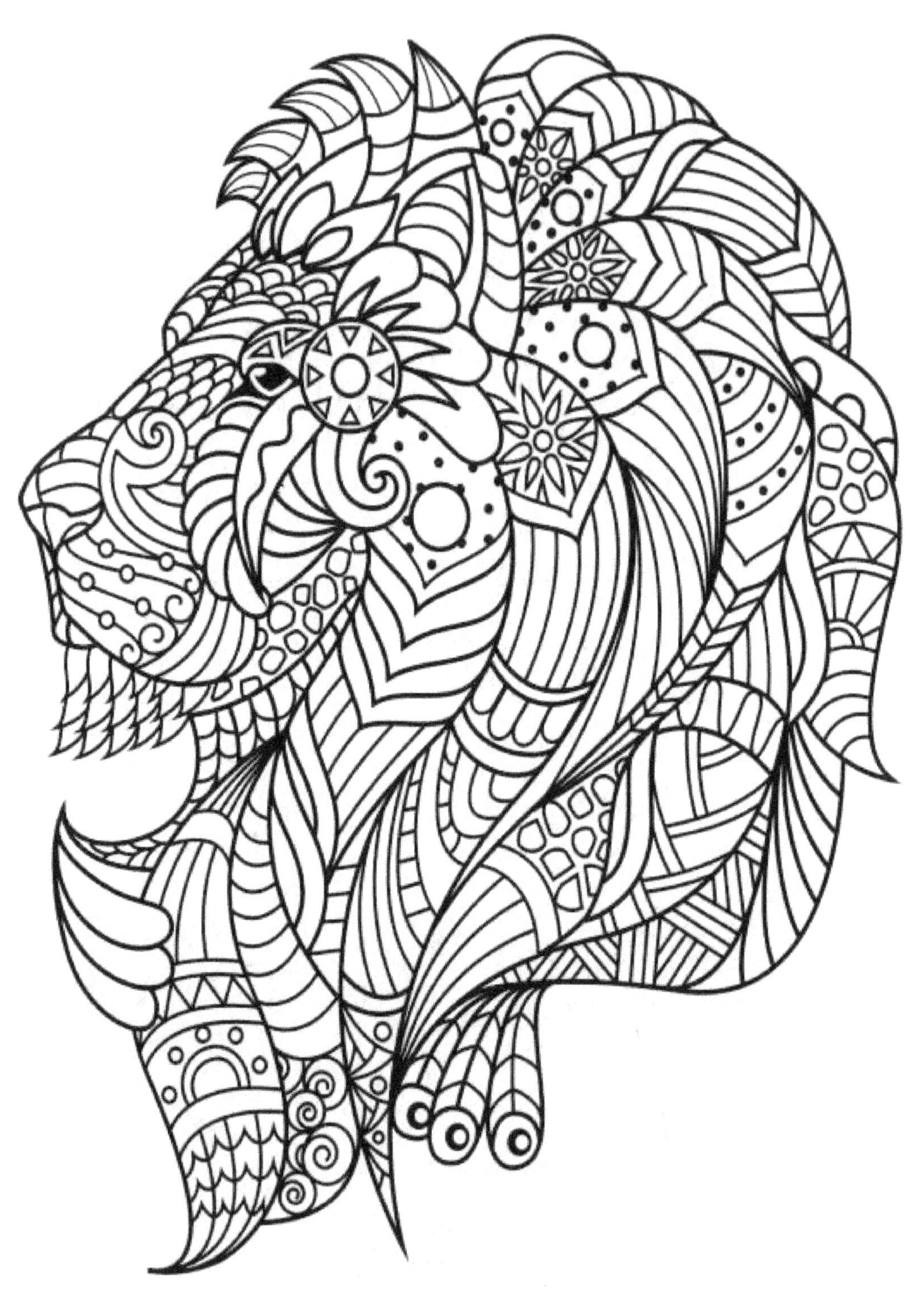

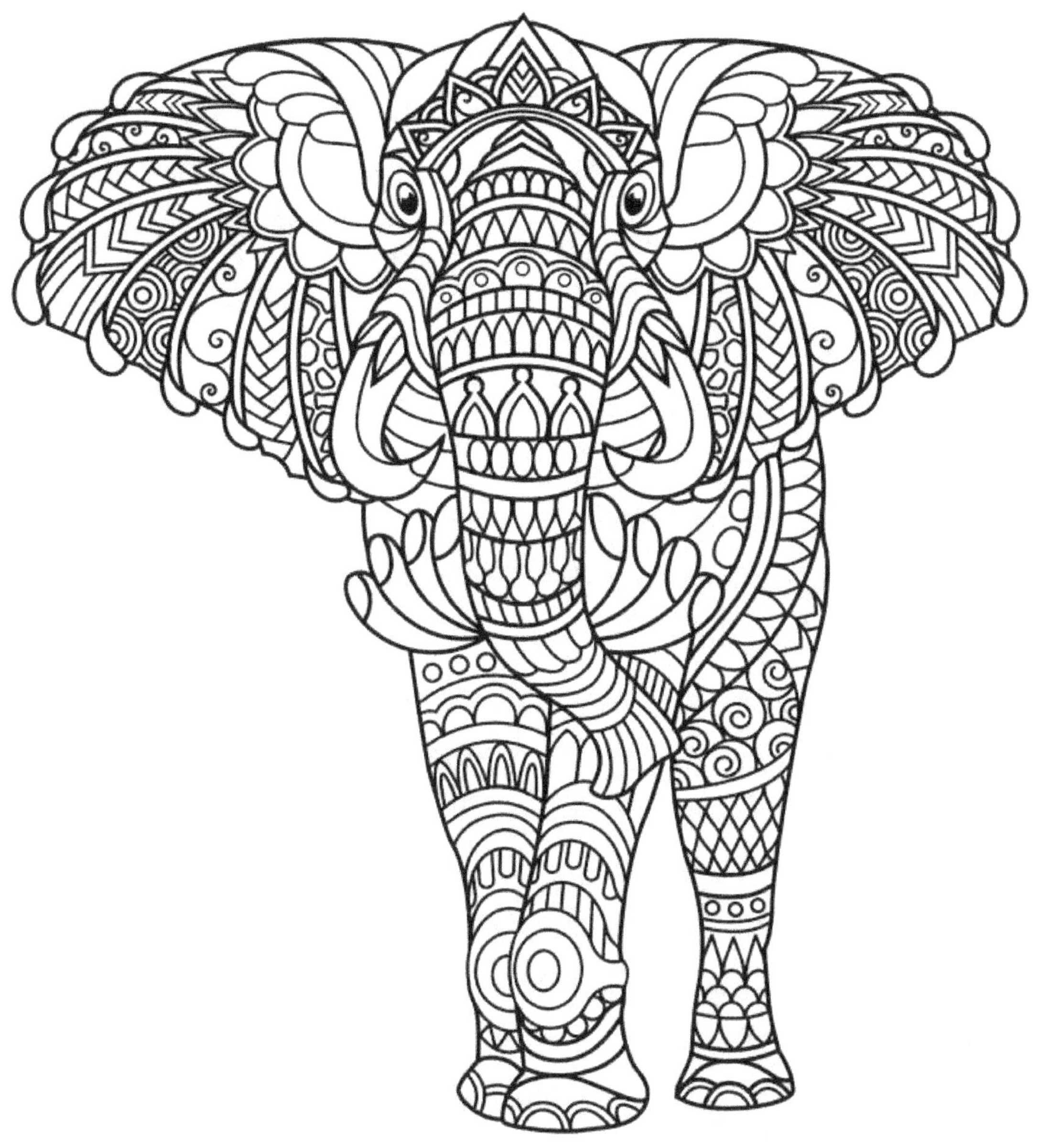

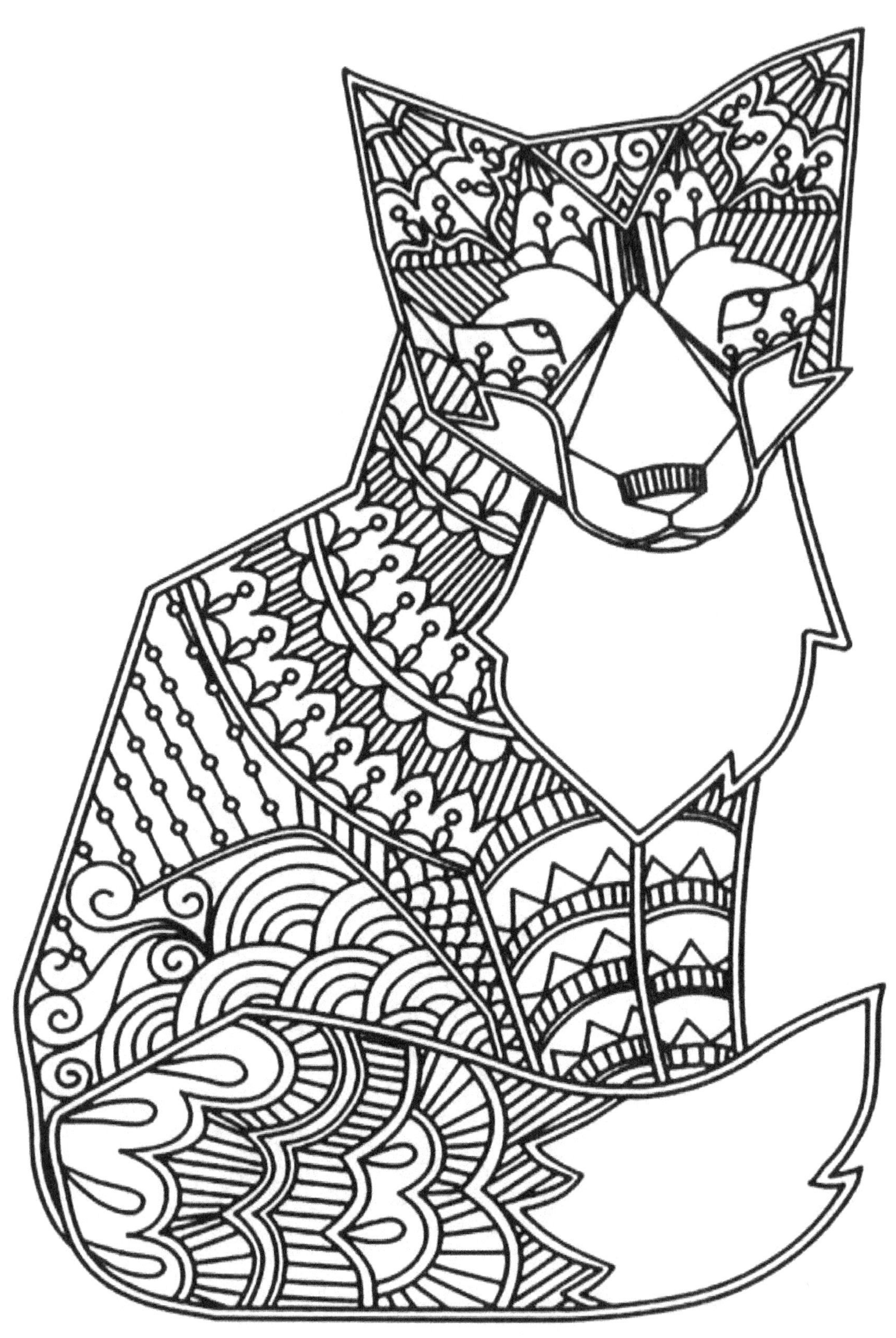

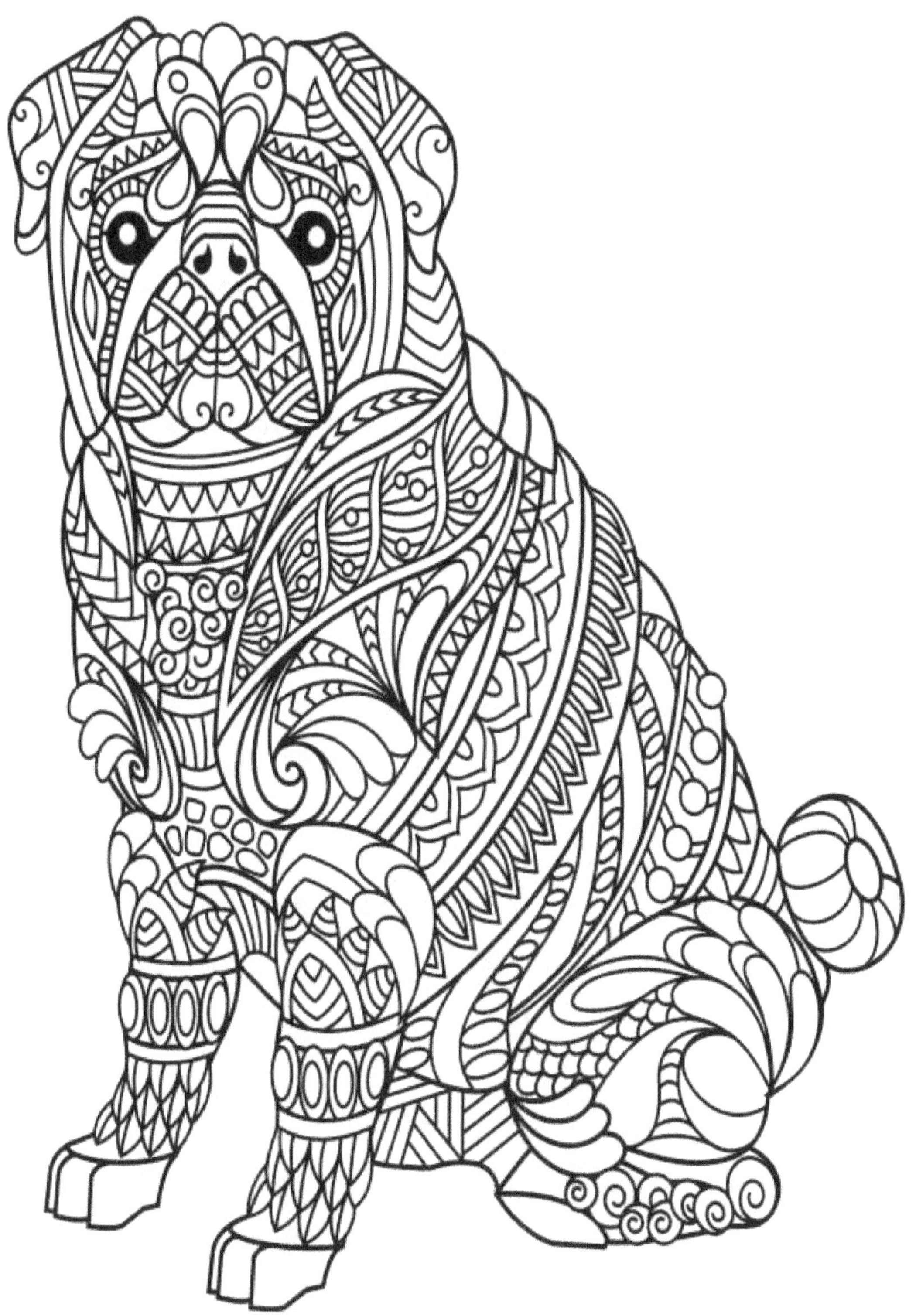

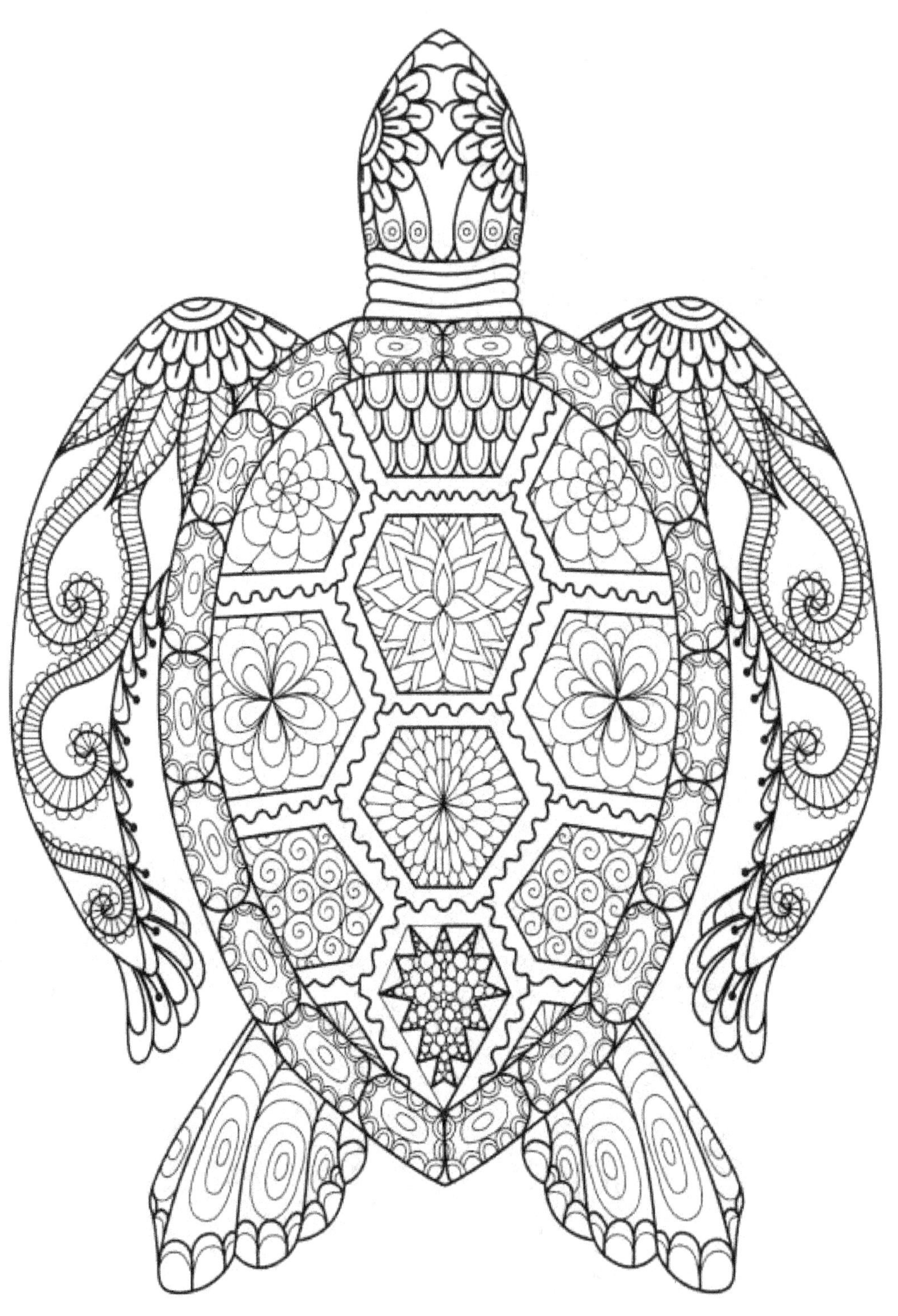

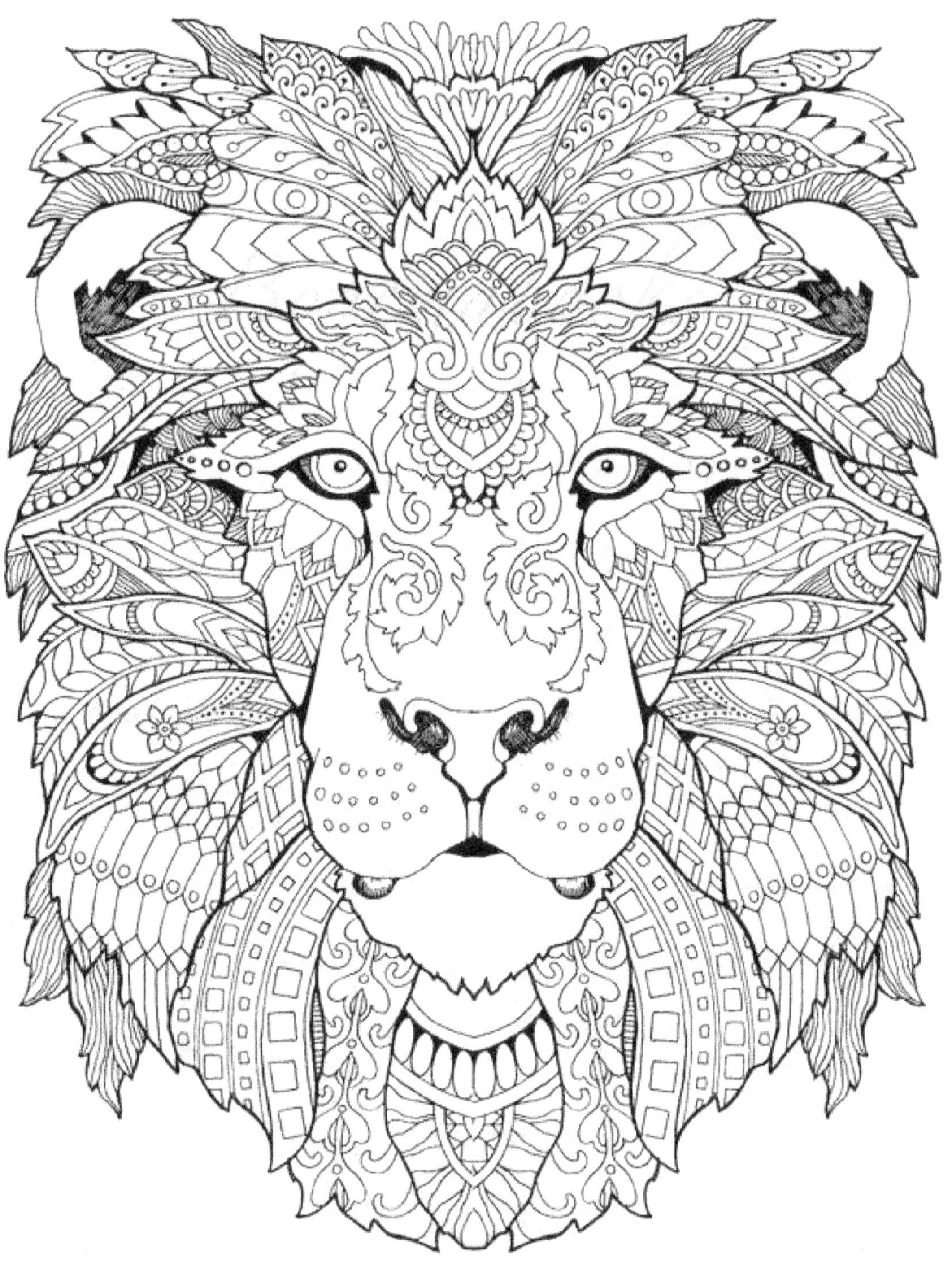

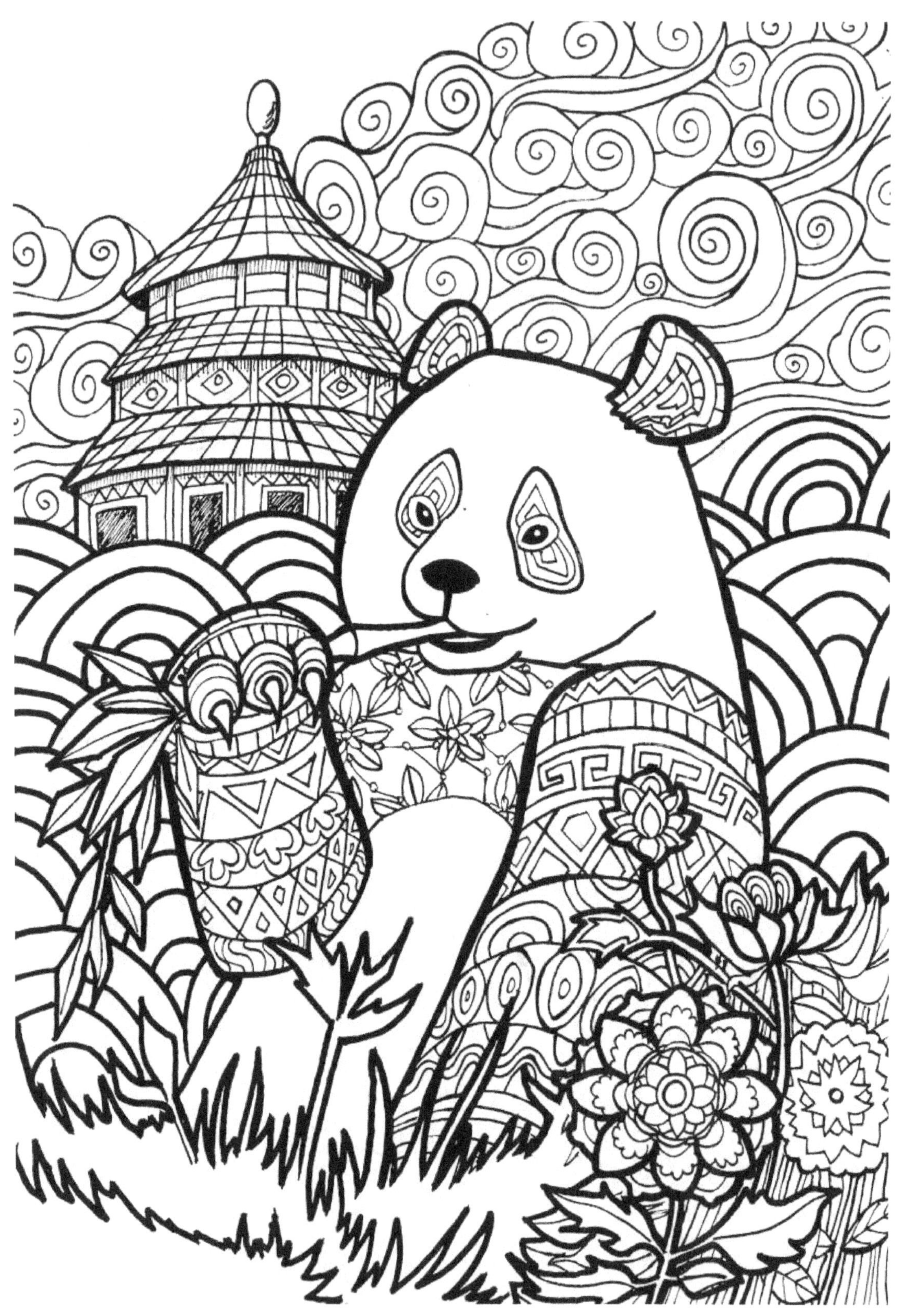

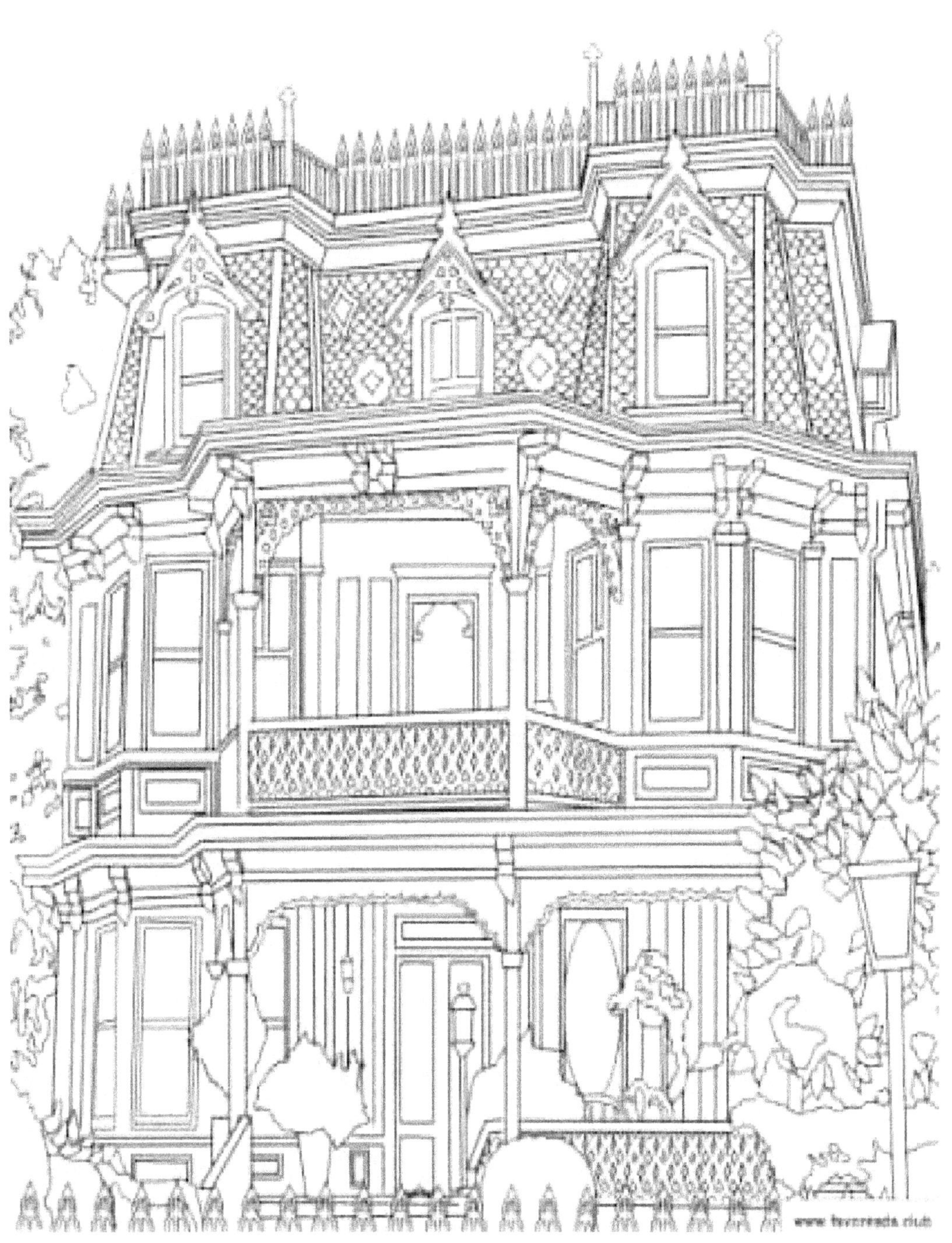

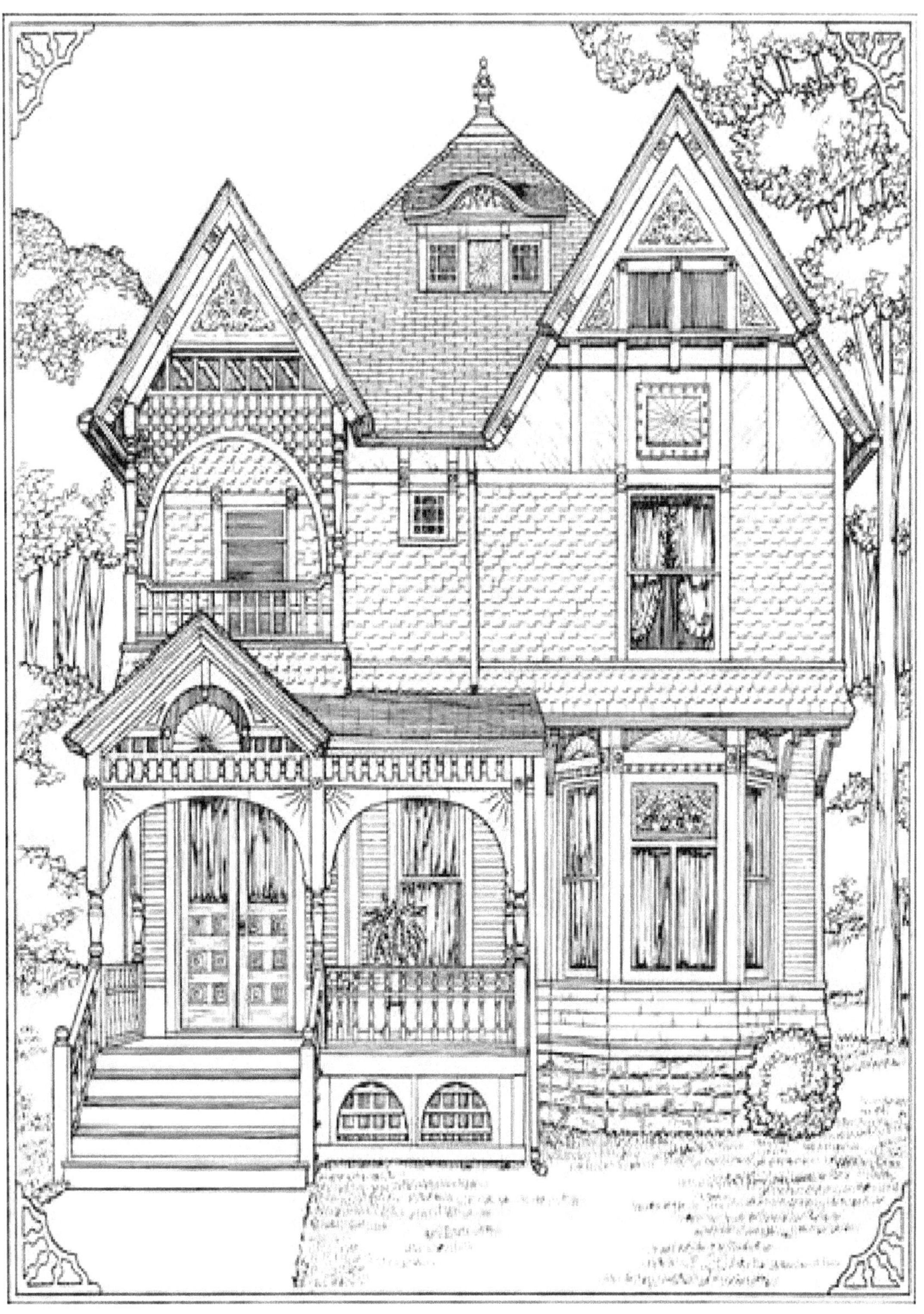

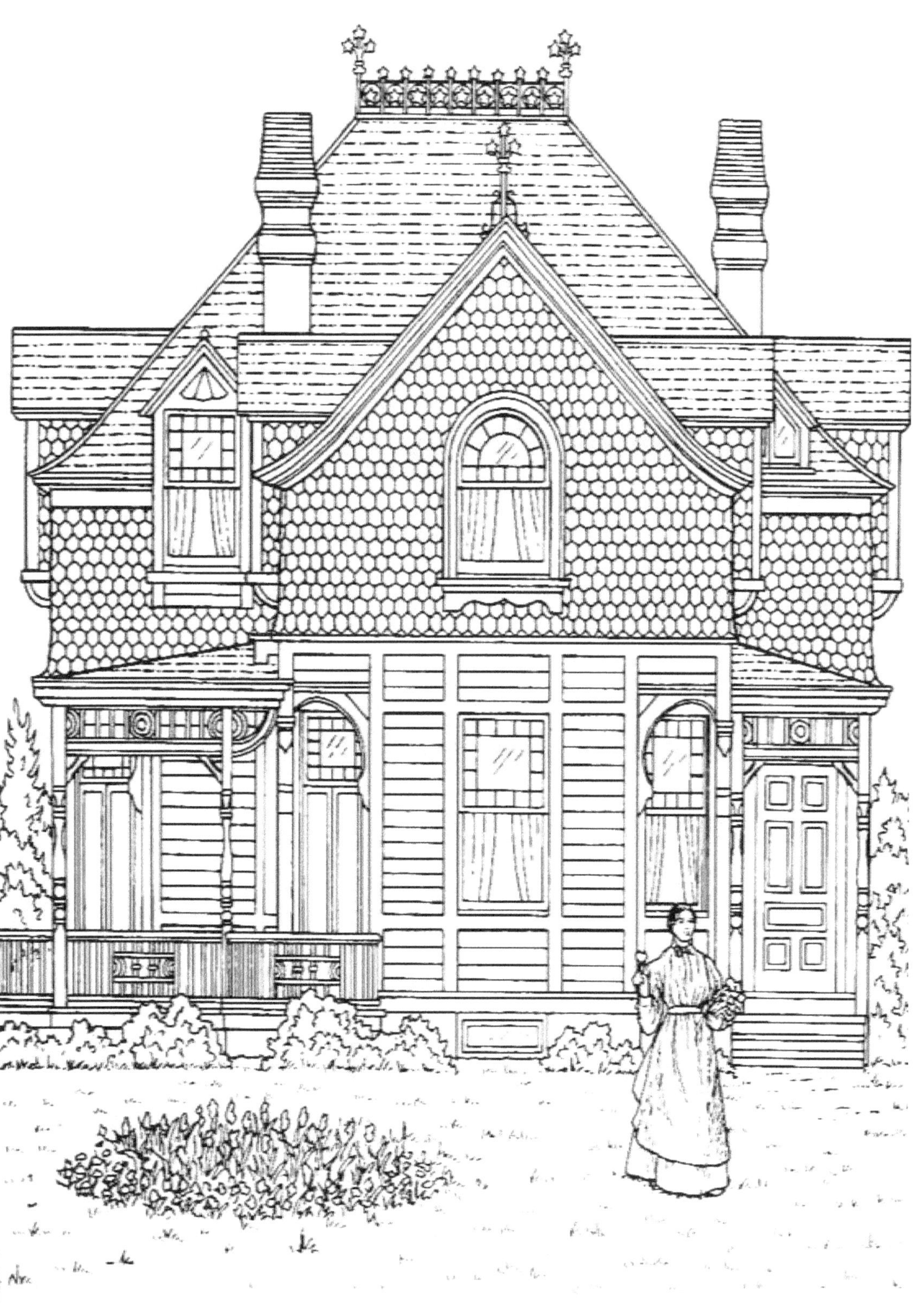

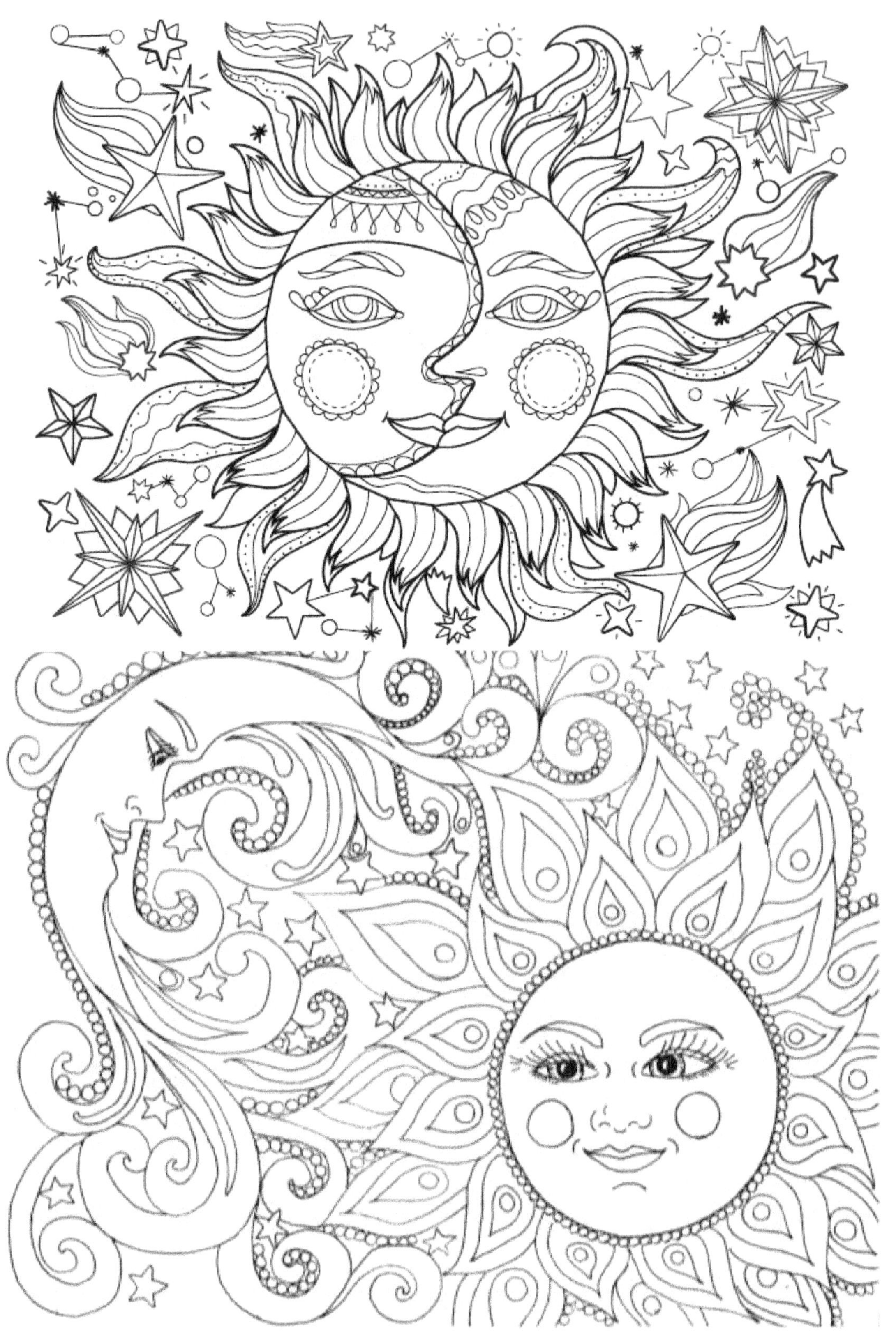

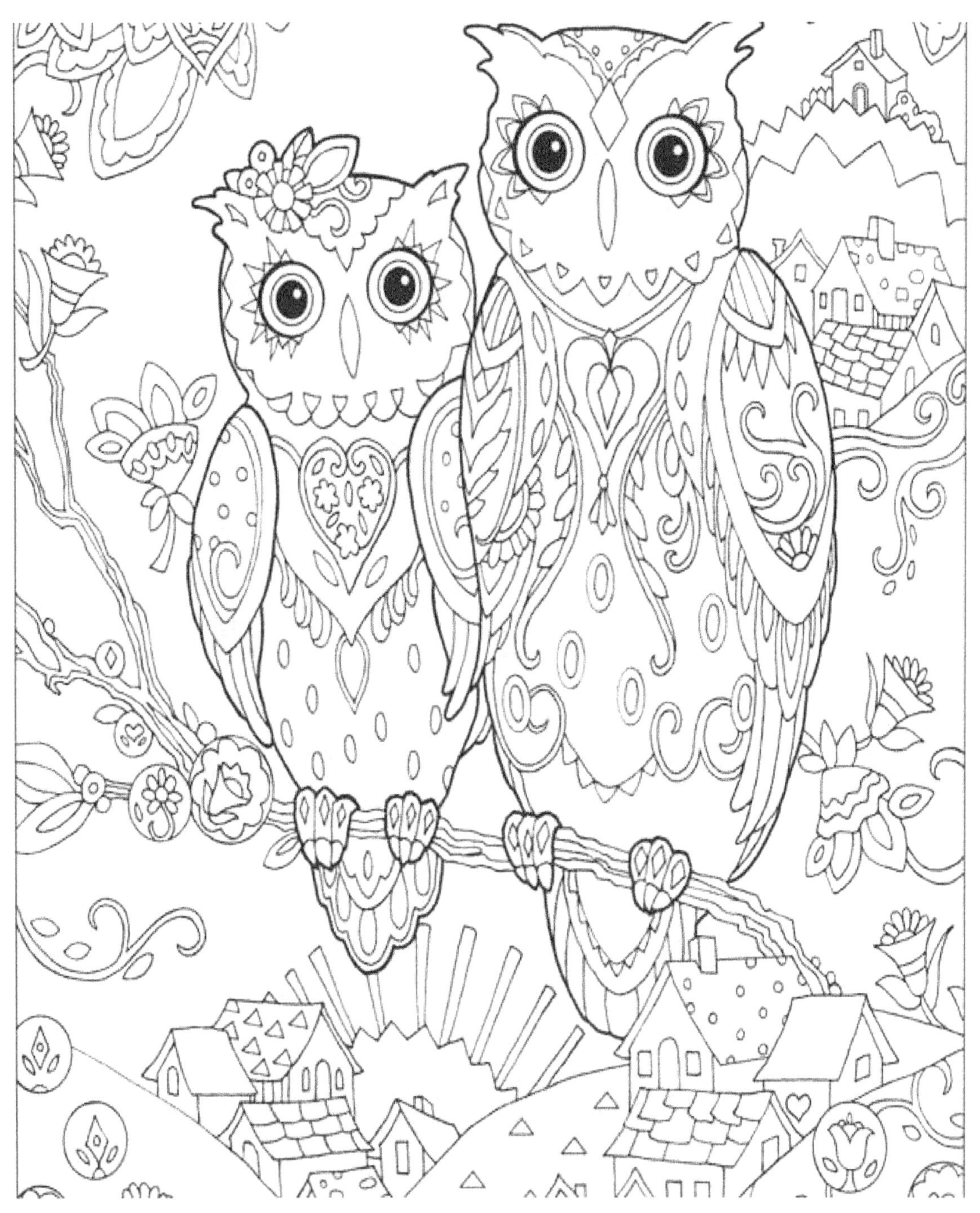

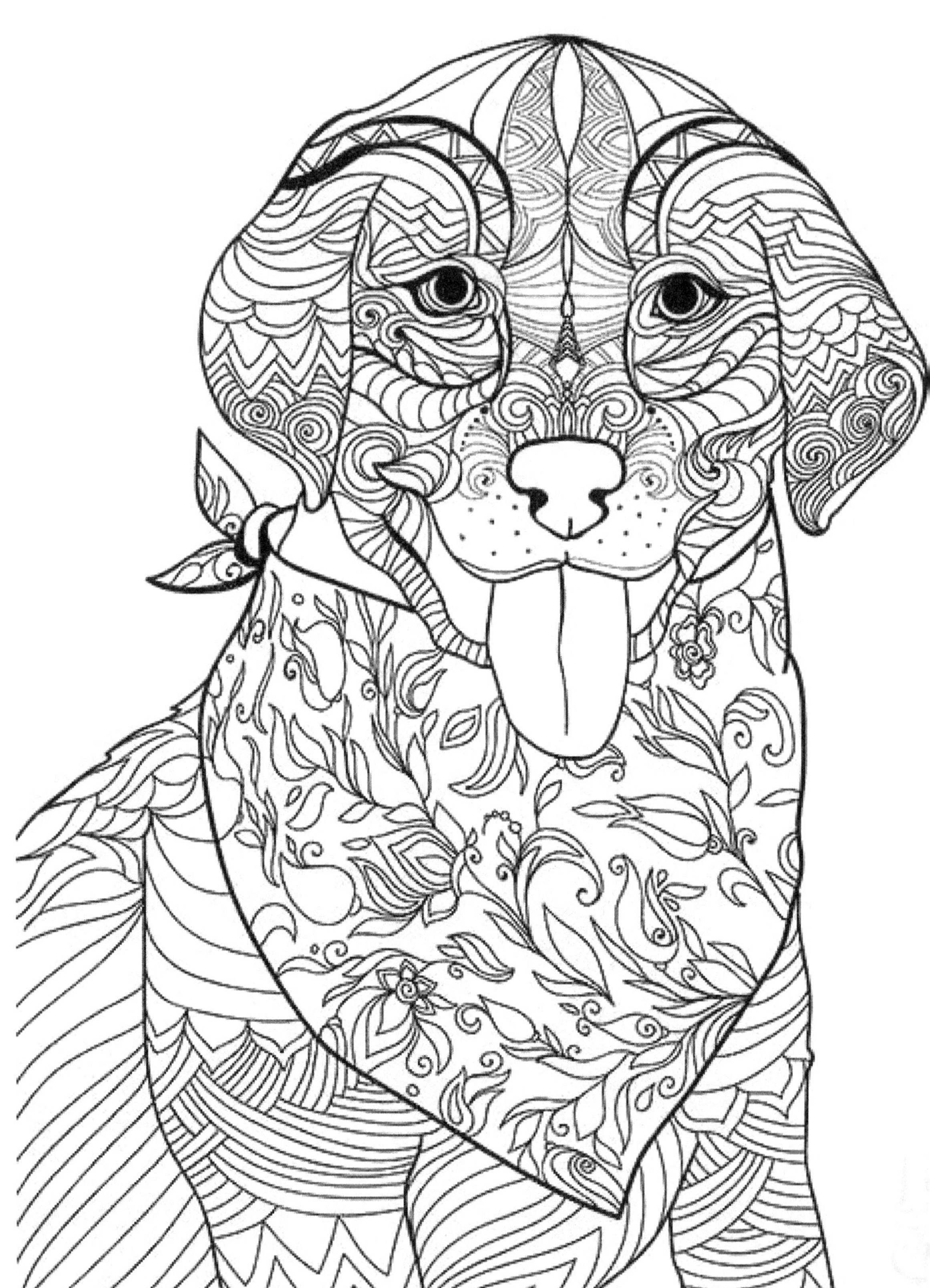

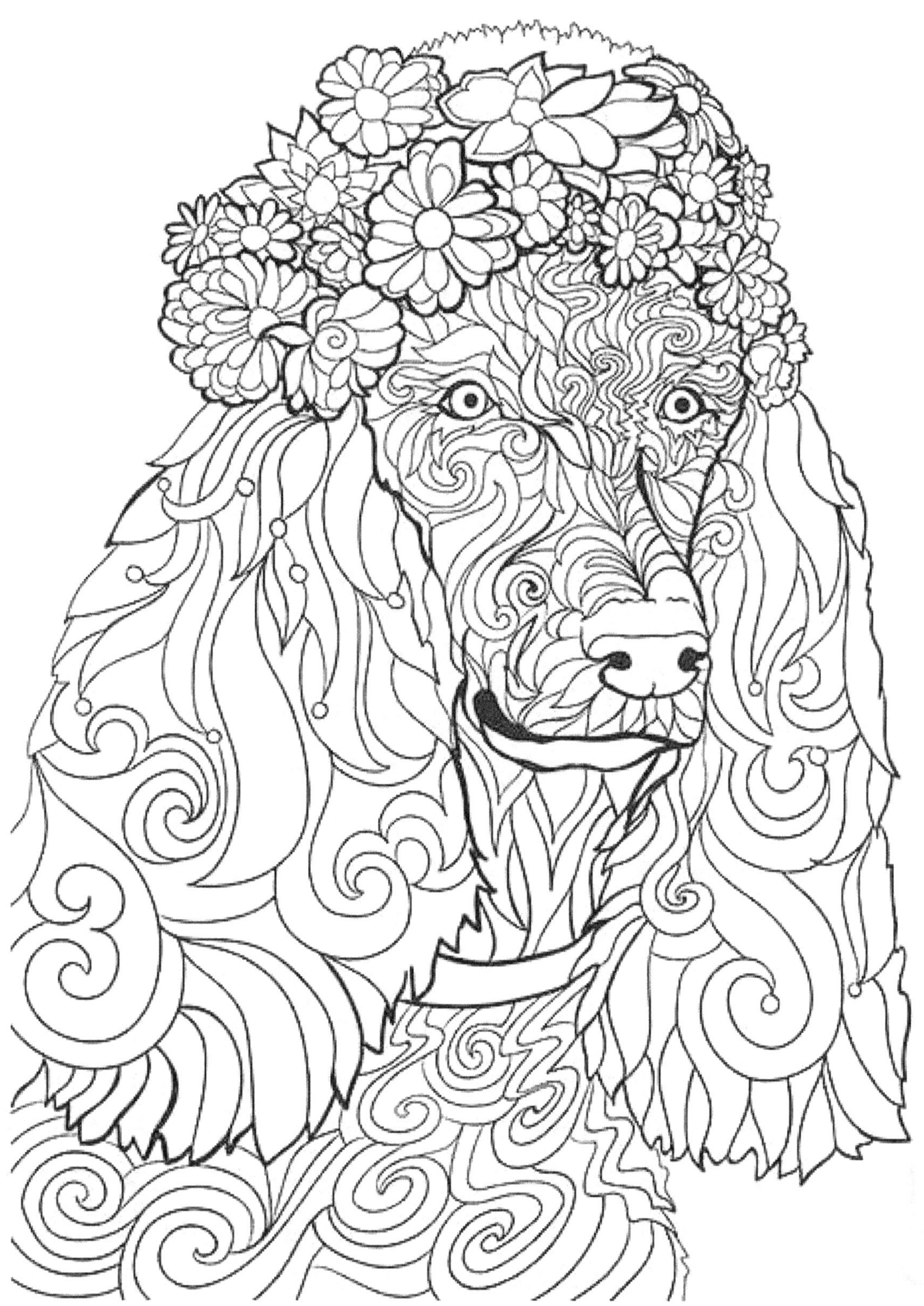

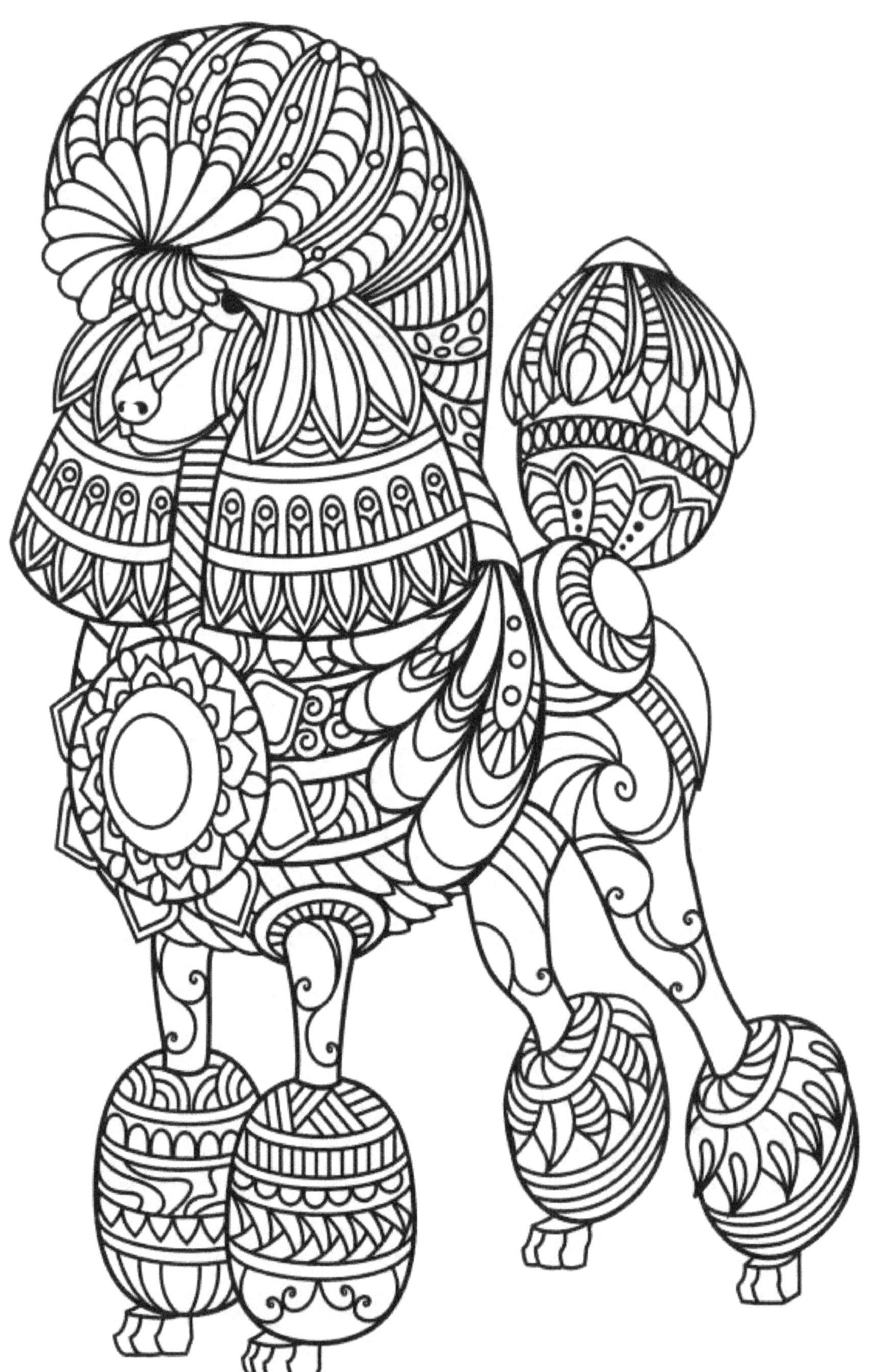

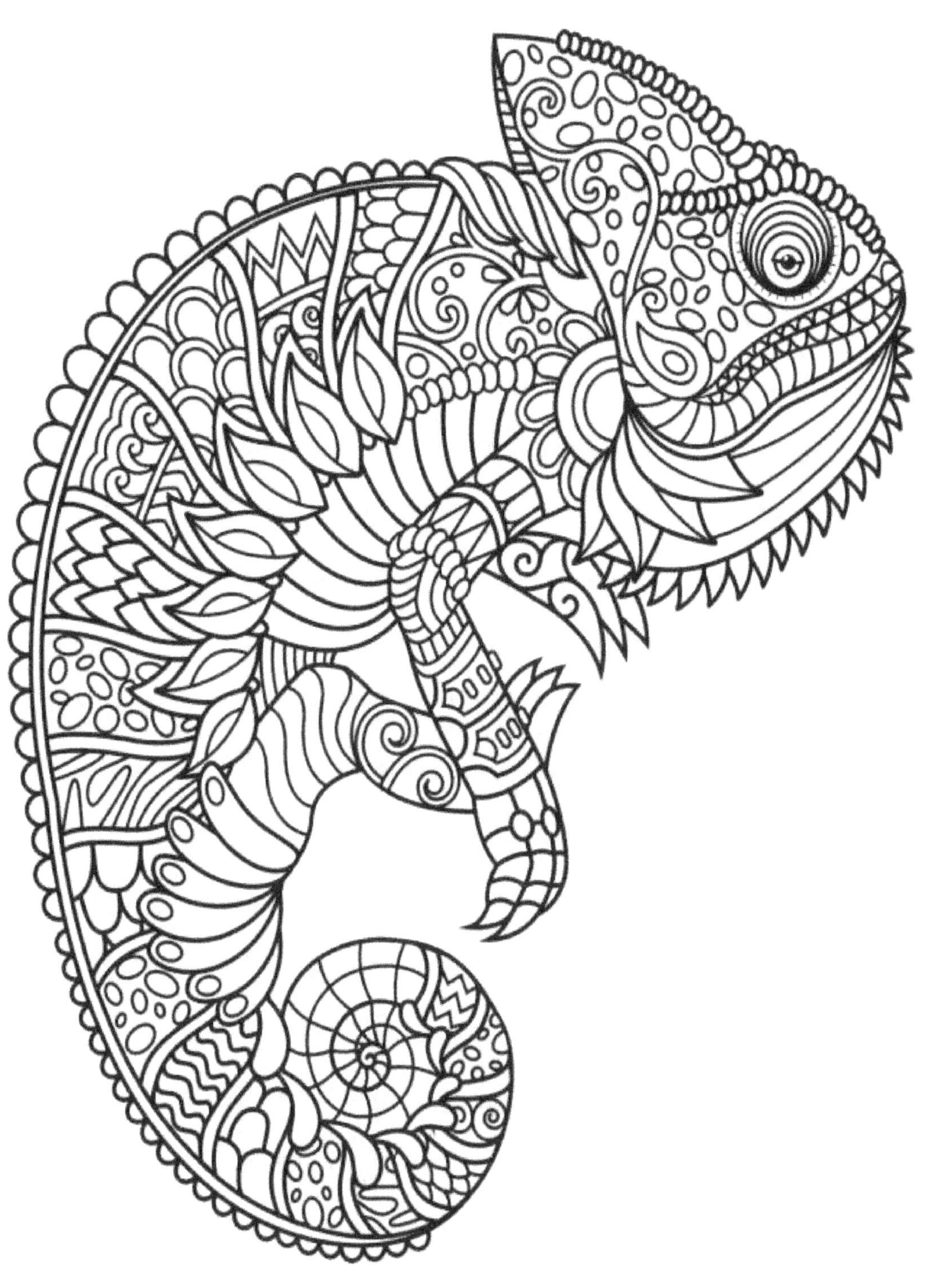

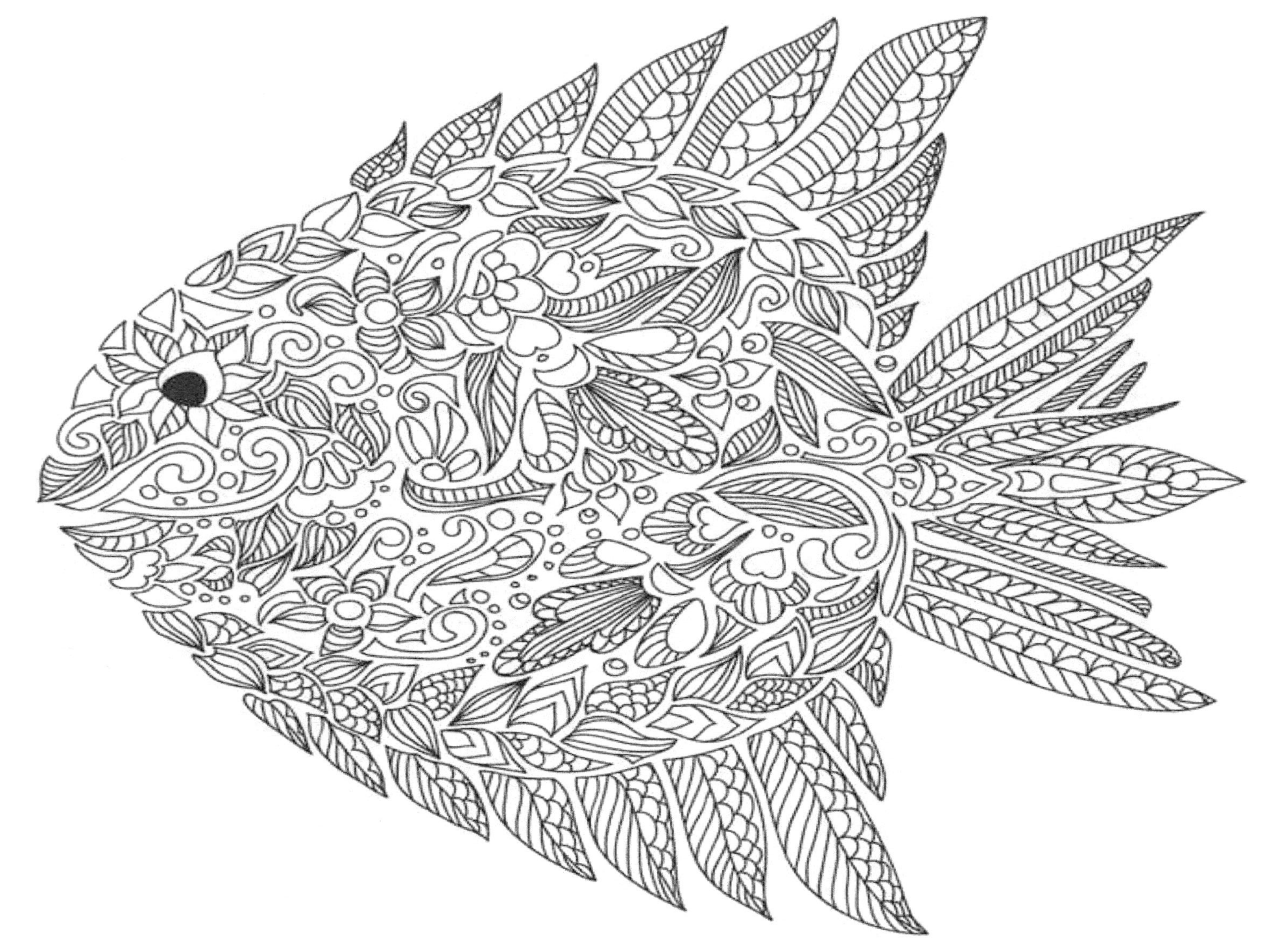